PART 1

STAGE HYPNOSIS-MY WAY

By

Terry Stokes, Sr.

To Doron)
God Bless)

COPYRIGHT 2018

This manuscript is dedicated to the new generation of stage hypnotists in the sincere hope that the profession enriches their lives as much as it has my own. When the torch was passed to me by Jack Berry he gave me a final piece of advice; "respect this profession and it will provide you with anything life has to offer. Abuse it and it will destroy you." Break-a-leg my friends!

CONTENTS PART ONE

PART TWO - Understanding Hypnosis

Part Two begins on page 123

INTRODUCTION

Over the years, I have watched 'trainers' teaching this art that I love and today there are literally hundreds teaching it. Rather than just comment on what I think is wrong with what is being taught, I decided it would be more productive to just do it right. Online, I have watched so called professionals bicker about who is the best and who said what about whom. This book is not one about ego; it is about methods that have been tried, fire tested and proven sound. I invite you to sample them and hope that in some small way I am able to contribute to the profession that has provided me with such a wonderful life. One of the things I found wrong with many training programs, my own included, is that SO much material is thrown at you that it is almost impossible to absorb it all. I went back to the way I learned.... a little at a time. If at every performance I could make my show just a little better, then in no time at all it would be the best. For example, imagine you just added 5 new routines a month to your show. In just one year, you have 60 extra bits at your disposal. You should only do about 7 or 8 major bits per show, so now you have 7 completely different shows, making it even easier to tailor the show to various audiences. If you fix just one mistake or problem a week, in a year your show will be unrecognizable from where it is now. You will discover as your show gets better, the checks get bigger. This book is designed to help you progress at your own pace. Not so fast that you are overwhelmed, but at a steady continuous pace towards excellence. You will receive new different lessons and tips in every chapter, so as you progress, the new material will just serve to build a more solid foundation. So, as Jonathan Livingston Seagull might say....

" Let's begin with level flight."

CHAPTER ONE

Why You Should Write Your Own Show

I saw my first hypnosis show in 1968. I was a student at the University of Georgia on spring break in Atlanta Georgia. Jack Berry was performing at a club called Earls Place just outside of Atlanta. I was blown away. There was no way that what I was seeing could possibly be real. I was back at the club every night for the next two weeks. He had different people on stage with him every night, so I thought to myself, "He was either making a fortune and could afford a cast of hundreds... or it must be real." Seemingly, at the drop of a word, Jack Berry had ordinary people doing extraordinary things. Singing, dancing, forgetting their own names, thinking they were movie stars. To say I was enthralled is an understatement. About two weeks into my skeptical investigation, I went on stage with Jack and became a believer. When I returned to school, I changed my major and began my lifelong quest to learn everything I could about hypnosis. Several years later when I decided to learn stage hypnosis, I sought out the man who had originally captured my attention, Jack Berry, who was known as "Mr. Hypnosis".

 For the first few years after seeing Jack perform, I attended at least 20 other hypnosis shows featuring a variety of hypnotists whose names I cannot even recall. They were all doing poor versions of Jack Berry's show. They were doing the same routines and jokes as Jack Berry but they just were not as funny. I assumed it was simply because I had seen it before. When I finally caught up with Jack, to my delight, I discovered his show was just as funny as it had been years earlier. When I asked him about it, his answer was short and simple. He said, "My stuff is funny because I wrote it. I created it. When other people do my material, they are just saying the words and, in many cases, do not even really understand why it is funny." He told me that as a performer, you can never truly take pride in doing someone else's material because you know deep down that you are a thief. I was able to persuade Jack to teach me his craft. He agreed to teach me but first elicited a promise that I would always be original. I could not do his material but he would teach me to create my own. 45 years later I am proud to say I have kept that promise. I have seen other hypnotists do material that I wish I had created, material that I would love to do, but if I cannot honestly say it is mine, I will not do it. On two occasions I have liked the bit so much that I approached the originator and offered to give them any two of my routines in return for their permission to use one of theirs. Anthony Cools, a very talented and original performer agreed, and whenever I do the bit, I tell the audience where it came from. The other hypnotist told me he had stolen the bit from someone else so I have never done it. At a show I attended recently, the performer came over and asked me how I liked his show. You need to understand...I am an asshole and will speak my mind. I told him I had not seen his show, I had just watched him do my show mixed with Ben Vandermead's show and topped off with a little bit of Anthony Cools' show, and the only thing I saw that he could claim as his own was his name. I later learned that the name was not even his. In a bit of a huff, he said everybody does everybody else's material, that's the way this business works. **That is not the way this business works.** If you are going to claim it as your show, then make it your show. I cannot make you be original or even teach you how to be creative in these pages. I can and will share with you the thought process that went into creating some of my material. I will give you some tips to force yourself into being original and as a side effect keep you from ever becoming bored doing a show. I can't stop you from doing my material but I hope to convince you that the pride you will gain from creating your own stuff will far surpass the slight joy you get from undeserved laughs. I cannot make you a great performer, but I can teach you how and why a hypnosis show works. This understanding alone will multiply your value as a performer tenfold. It will give you confidence to do a show under any circumstance, in any condition. Understanding the "why" gives you the confidence to dominate any stage.

If you, as a stage hypnotist, learned your craft by memorizing an induction and how to do certain routines, I submit that you are an actor merely reciting lines and not deserving the right to call it "your show". If you want it to be "YOUR" show, here are some basic rules to follow.

1. **BE YOURSELF** - My style is very laid back and charming. I want everyone to like me. That is who I am. One of my former partners, Michael Johns, is very caustic. He seems not to care if you like him or not, and yet his is one of the funniest and best hypnosis shows I have ever seen. His style works for him and my style works for me...total opposites yet they both work. Incidentally, off stage Michael is one of the kindest and

loving souls I have ever known. Our styles work for us because we are not trying to be anyone else. One of my very best friends, Mark Yuzuik learned to do a hypnosis show from me. When he was trying to be me, he was only OK. When he discovered who he was and let that personality come out on stage, overnight he became great. That overnight transformation actually took several years but when it happened, Mark was suddenly one of the very best in the business. You must **Decide who you are.**

2. <u>**UNDERSTANDING A HYPNOSIS SHOW**</u> - A hypnosis show is unlike any other show in the world. It is also the most difficult to master. It is not about training your voice like a singer. It is not about mastering timing like a comedian. It is not about practicing moves like a dancer. It is not about learning lines like an actor. It is not about learning tricks like the magician. AND IT IS NOT ABOUT PARROTING ROUTINES YOU SAW SOMEONE ELSE DO!! All of these things are important and will make you a better performer.... but you have chosen to do something much more difficult. A STAGE HYPNOTIST RECOGNIZES AND BRINGS OUT TALENT IN TOTAL STRANGERS....HE INSTILLS CONFIDENCE AND DIRECTS THE ATTENTION AND ACTIONS OF INDIVIDUALS HE HAS NEVER MET. HE

CONTROLS CHAOS AND MAKES IT APPEAR AS IF HE IS DOING NOTHING AT ALL. Ask yourself why why did you attend your first hypnosis show. Why does anyone go to a hypnosis show? They go because they have heard it was fun. Friends told them. They stumbled on it at fairgrounds. Why do people go to any kind of show? Somehow, they got the idea it was going to be fun. Your job is to fulfill their expectations. No one goes to your show to educated. Now ask, why do people volunteer to be in a show?

A. They want to be a star

B. They want to prove you are a fake

C. They just want to try something new

There are no other reasons. If you take someone on stage who you know is going to challenge you...you are going to lose. Do you want someone who just wants to try something new? They are going to be your most analytical people and therefore not your best subjects. You need to understand that **most people want to be a star**.... they want to be an entertainer. They want to get up on stage and make people laugh and enjoy themselves. You give them a chance to do something they have dreamed of doing their entire life. If they

make an ass of themselves, it is your fault. Now if you want to be really good at what you are doing,
you won't let them make an ass of themselves, you will make them a star. As a matter of fact, your main job is to make your volunteers look good.

SETTING THE STAGE - You should always use straight back chairs in a straight line or semi-circle. The main thing is that every chair can be seen from any place in the room. This is of course under ideal circumstances and some places that just will not be possible but always make sure you check for maximum visibility. The chairs should be touching. You want your chairs touching and not tied together. One of
the reasons for not tying them together is so that you can remove extra chairs after you pick your subjects. You want them touching so that the people sitting in them can feel the person next to them responding to suggestions. Remember, it is a 'Follow the Leader' show. When they feel the person next to them raising their arms, theirs will begin to rise too.

LIGHTING - Of course there is the obvious 'light the stage so that the audience can see' but do you understand that this is the least of importance of reasons for lighting the stage? What I am about to tell you is not understood by 95% of the hypnotist performing today and it can make the absolute difference between a great show and a dud. It can make the difference between keeping all of your volunteers or just 10%. Correct lighting is the most powerful yet subtle tool you have in your arsenal. First, let's look at the way most people, probably even you, do it. You make sure the stage is bright so everyone can be seen. Then when you begin your induction, you slowly fade the lights. Sounds simple enough so what could be wrong with that? This is how to make the lighting work for you. The light should be focused to effectively blind everyone on stage to the audience. They should only be able to see you in front of them. In a later section we will discuss why you only want 8 to 10 people on stage, but for now, please just take my word for it. When lights are available, they should be focused so as to effectively blind people sitting in the chairs to anything beyond the stage edge. When you tell them to look into your eyes, they will actually be staring directly into the light so that when you say, "in a moment your eyes will begin to burn and water, THEY WILL FIND THEIR OWN EYES STARTING TO BURN AND WATER, exactly as you said, exactly when you said. Now you tell them to close their eyes because that will make them feel better. when they close their eyes, they do feel better. Once again, you said it and it happened. Even with their eyes closed, the volunteers are still aware of the bright lights. If when you tell them to "SLEEP", the lights suddenly go out or dim 75%, it give them the a feeling of sudden dis- orientation , and if they were not quite under, they will be now. This simple trick will boost your success percentage 20 fold.

GETTING VOLUNTEERS - Many people have learned to do a show from Ormand Mcgill's book The Encyclopedia of Stage Hypnosis. This is a wonderful book if you are doing theatre shows for sold out houses. Most shows today are in clubs or casino showrooms. In a theatre, you can get away with doing a 10, 12 or even 15-minute induction. In a night club you can expect audience cooperation and silence for a maximum of 4 minutes. After that they lose interest and you will spend the first half hour after the induction trying to win the audience back. Your induction should be no longer than 3 to 3 1/2 min. Less than 3 minutes is not believable. More about that later. In a theater setting, it is permissible to have 25 volunteers on stage. In a night club, I take 10 volunteers and usually keep 8. There are basically two methods for getting volunteers on stage. The first, which is used by most performers, is to simply say something to the effect of, "come on up, be my guest" and then allow people to rush to the stage. This technique is the most used because it is the easiest and requires no thought on your part. I do not use it for the following reasons:

- In a night club situation, you are going to get the drunkest people in the room.

- Most of your volunteers will be about the same age (I will explain why this is an issue in a moment).

- You are going to get groups of friends all sitting together (also an issue).

- You are relinquishing control and inviting chaos into your show.

In most cases, your audience is made up of a wide variety and types of people. Every person in the room should be able to relate to at least one person on your stage. You need a variety of ages, ethnicity, and cultural background. You want every audience member thinking, "that could be me up there". It is this connection that allows the audience to actually care about what is happening on stage. Also, there should be people from all areas of the room. If several of your volunteers are from the same table, that looks suspicious to your audience. It is important that people who know each other, or are friends, are not seated together on stage. They will always be more concerned with how their friend is doing than listening to you. When you allow your volunteers to rush to the stage, then you are giving away control of your show. I prefer to use the technique whereby I ask, "For those who would like to be the stars of the show, or experience the power of hypnosis" to simply raise their hands. I then point and select the people who come on stage. In this way I am able to select a wide variety of people. I can ignore the drunks and people who might, for any number of reasons be undesirable for a show. I am able to direct them to sit where I want and not have to waste time rearranging the stage. I am also able to dispel the idea that I am using plants by simply pointing to some area and saying, "you have already done it, let's give other people a chance." Most importantly…I have maintained control of my show!

YOU AS THE DIRECTOR - As a comedy stage hypnotist, you should think of yourself as the director of a great production. Think of your show like a movie. You are the director. You choose the stars. You assign the roles. You direct the action. I stress, you are not the star but a very important supporting player. What would the production look like if the director put all of his actors in a room without a script and yelled action. There would be chaos which is exactly the way many shows look. You do not expect your actors to be talented screen writers and masters of improvisation. As the director, you set the scene and give direction. Remember the old home movies where the camera suddenly landed on your aunt Betty and all the contortions, she went through to keep from being filmed. Funny for a second, but only a second.... BUT... tell her to stick out her tongue or give a sexy wink and you have a scene. Don't expect your actors to be clever.... some are clever...but they are few and far between. When you say, you who I am touching, upon awakening such and such will happen, what you are actually saying is, now in this next scene..da da da da da. You are the director. Now let's expand this idea of your show being like a movie. Why does a director look through squared fingers to shape a scene? He wants to see what the camera sees. Your audience is your camera. When you are doing a bit, you have to consider how the audience sees it. That's why you move to different sides of your volunteers to give a better camera shot.

If in your movie all of your scenes are close ups with a single person doing dialog, the movie gets boring fast. If all the scenes are panoramic, that also gets boring. The movie need dialogue between actors. It needs monologues. It needs wide screen action shots. Just as an artful blend of shots can change a boring home movie into a theatrical Masterpiece, so can you change a boring show in to something unforgettable. There should be plot twist and callbacks. What? You don't have enough material to do all of that. You should and you will. You should ask yourself what kind of scenes do you want in your movie, or what kind of skits should you do. There are several types of skits.

Types of skits

- Group skits...those are your panoramic shots. The orchestra or funny movie are group skits.

- Individual skits.... working with one person only. In an individual bit, you want the person to do as little as possible with the maximum effect. I think it was Marlon Brando who said, the secret to great acting is not to act.

- Interactive skits.... involving 2 or more people. When Mary sneezes, John Farts. One action causes another.

- Audience involvements skits....When you hear applause, you will stand and wave to your fans.

- Throw aways.... filler material

There are several ways to set up a skit. Done properly, the suggestion itself should get almost as much laughter as the skit itself does. Tell a story about how you came up with the idea. Talk about something everyone has in common and wonder what would happen if you made a small change or put it into a different situation.

CANNED SHOWS - Most hypnotists do canned or memorized shows because doing it that way requires no thought. If you learned to do a hypnosis show by memorizing certain words and scripts, the first thing I will tell you is "START OVER". You should know the 'why" of every single thing you say and do in a show. Begin by understanding that you are not doing a lecture. You are not being paid to educate about hypnosis. You are not being paid to convince anyone of anything. You are there to entertain an audience. Your goal should be to connect with every single person in that audience. You might on rare occasions have a "bad" audience but in most cases, they were not bad, you just read them wrong and didn't make the connection. If you are doing a canned show then you are demanding that the audience conform and agree to your idea of what is funny when it should be the other way around. Look at the age range of your crowd. Look at the part of the country they are in. How are they dressed? Are they couples or singles? How are you going to make your memorized presentation fit any audience you might encounter? The answer is, YOU CAN'T! People everywhere like to laugh, but what they laugh AT varies and is constantly changing. People do not come to see a hypnosis show to become educated on the subject. They want to laugh. They want to be the star of the show, or they want to know the stars of the show. They want to be amazed. They do not care about Anton Mesmer or how many degrees you might have. They want to be entertained, so do your job. To illustrate this point, I would like to relate a valuable learning experience I went through. Several years ago, I was invited to take my comedy hypnosis show to Hong Kong. My first concern was the language barrier. I was assured that more people spoke English in Hong Kong than in California. That turned out to be true. The first night we were sold out. I got great volunteers who followed every suggestion perfectly. No one laughed. The applauded politely and there were a few chuckles… but nothing like I was accustomed to. The next night was a repeat of this but only a half full room. I went to the agent and told him I didn't think my show was going to be successful here. These people did not get it. I knew my stuff was funny but they just didn't get it. He said he could cancel the rest of the date but suggested first that I take the weekend and go see some other comedy shows in town. The Steve Martin movie, "THE JERK" was playing in town. I loved this film and found something new to laugh at every time I saw it. I went to the movie, but instead of watching the movie, I watched and listened to the audience. They laughed at different things. What I thought was hysterical barely got a chuckle from this audience. I watched for the things that made them laugh and tried to understand why. That night I figured out how to change my material to target their funny bones. For example, one bit that I had just started doing in the United States that always worked was the little girl with makeup bit. Basically, I told a guy that he was a six-year-old little girl. Mommy was off at the store and he/she had found Mommies' purse. This purse contained all the magical wonderful things that made Mommy so pretty. It contained the eye shadow, the lipstick, the makeup. Wouldn't it be fun to make up just like Mommy? The guy would apply the makeup and usually make a big mess like you would expect a six-year-old to do. The Hong Kong audience did not laugh. Analyzing this routine, I realized that for an Asian child to take Mommies' purse without permission was unthinkable. I made a simple change to the set up. Mommy has been teaching you to apply makeup. She bought you your very own purse so that you can practice. Mommy would be so proud if you learned to how to do it now. The bit worked. The audience went wild. I made my material fit their culture. With these changes, I started getting nightly standing ovations and was held over for 16 weeks. The lesson here is not to expect any audience to conform to the routines you learned. You are there for them…. they are not there for you. If you adopt this attitude, and believe me, this is a necessary attitude for a stage hypnotist, you will find that you will grow your talents tenfold overnight.

CHAPTER TWO

YOU AS THE DIRECTOR

In chapter one, we talked about thinking of yourself as the director of a film masterpiece. Let's continue with that analogy. Think of the movies you have seen and enjoyed. If the scene was too dark and difficult to discern images you quickly lost interest. Darkness can set a mood, but too much darkness causes the viewer to lose interest. What about films that are all frantic, with the actors running about in pure chaos. Enjoyable? What about a movie that has no plot twists or even believable characters? It is certainly acceptable to make movies like this, but are they the type of films you want to make or would enjoy watching? I submit that you want to make a movie, or create a show, that can be enjoyed by everyone. A show that will be remembered and talked about because of its content and not because of its shock value. Anyone can turn on a camera and make a movie but to make a good movie you must start with structure. Anyone can memorize a script, recite it in front of people and call it a show. You need to ask yourself what story do you want to tell. It is important to decide this up front because this will determine the way you proceed. For example, do you want to be a "star" and demonstrate what a powerful person you are? There is nothing wrong with that if that is the direction you choose. If that **is** you, I suggest magic might be more suited to you, but there are many in hypnosis who choose this very direction. Perhaps you want to educate about hypnosis. If that is your direction, then your show structure will be entirely different. In another section we will talk about different structures for different types of show goals, but here I want to start with my favorite. For now, let's assume you want to present an entertainment experience that can be enjoyed by any audience. You want to the audience to leave knowing they have been truly entertained and respect you for giving them such a great experience. This begins with a quick attitude adjustment. Start with this. The people on stage with you are not your subjects. They are not your props. They are not your committee. They are your "STARS"! They are the people who will allow you to have the most amazing lifestyle imaginable. They will feed your family and buy you big cars and homes. When you realize and accept this fact and begin to treat them with the respect they deserve, your own status will soar. You are the director whose skill it is to get the maximum performance from your stars. The girl or guy helping you on stage is not your assistant or helper but your on-stage partner and should always be introduced as such. In this manuscript, I might refer to your assistant or your volunteers for ease of reference but would never introduce them publicly that way. Now you know who you will be working with, it is time to make them feel as "at home" on stage as you appear to be. I say "appear to" because despite appearances, you will always be scared. After thousands and thousands of shows, I am still terrified to walk on stage. That is the very thing will make you good; the fear that you might fail or disappoint an audience. **You should strive not to get rid of your butterflies but rather to teach them to fly in formation.** Make the fear work for you. Your apparent confidence puts your stars at ease. They must feel that everything is under control.

YOUR FIRST WORDS - So, now you take the stage and begin to speak. I am astounded by how many supposed professionals walk on stage and begin with, "how is everyone tonight?" To me, that is the sign of an amateur. Think about this for just a moment. Do you want everyone to shout out how they are feeling? If they do, can you hear or do you really care? Do you want to go to everyone individually and find out how they are doing? Do you care how everyone is doing? Your job is to make them better no matter how they are when you begin. You ask that stupid question just so you have something to say. Why not open with a positive statement. "Wow, good looking crowd, except maybe you sir" "Great to be here, as opposed to home...I'm married". Any positive statement and if you can make it funny, even better. Ask your questions later, but ask one person so it seems as if you actually care about the answer. Audience questions are used to train the audience to applaud not shout or to fill your awkward first moments in front of them. "By your applause, how many of you have seen a show like this before?" Do you see what you are doing? You are training your audience to communicate with you by clapping instead of shouting. Believe it or not, this will actually lower your number of hecklers. Your opening remarks should be brief and get a laugh. Unless this is a teaching seminar, your audience did not pay the cover charge or come in the room to be educated. They came to be entertained. Don't disappoint them in the first five minutes by spewing out how much you know about hypnosis. They don't care. **They do not care how much you know until they know how much you care.** Don't waste time telling everyone how much you know, demonstrate it by your attitude and confidence. Trust me...THEY DO NOT CARE! They are there to be entertained, so do your job.

I watched a video a few days ago where the hypnotist touted all of his hypnotic education and experience, and then in his first routine told the "Star" that their hand was stuck tight to their head. "It is stucker and stucker. The harder you pull, the more stucker it would be." My guess is that all his talk about his education went right out the window. Maybe mention that hypnosis is not like you expect and that everyone can be hypnotized and then demonstrate with a suggestibility test. You said it and then proved it...nothing to debate. Start getting your laughs while doing the suggestibility test. Two suggestibility tests are plenty. Don't keep doing test after test to fill time. That quickly becomes boring to the audience. If you make this demonstration serious with no laughs you are giving the idea that hypnosis is all serious. Your opening remarks or pre-talk have only one main purpose and that purpose is to make your audience like and respect you and have confidence in your abilities. It should make them want to be a part of your world by coming up on your stage. In my show, I take this physiological set up even farther. I do not even go onstage until my "STARS" are seated. I come on through the audience and do all my opening bits in front of the stage. I am out in the audience with the people. Later, when I invite them up, my on-stage partner seats them and then goes back into the wings. They are uncomfortable sitting there alone because they are not sure what to do. When I say I think I will come up there and join you, they feel relief and comfort and they are happy that I am there to be their leader. This is a very subtle suggestion to set the stage for them accepting my leadership. Put yourself for a moment in the seats of the stars. Think how you would be feeling. I discovered this little tidbit when I was a volunteer in another hypnotist show and was listening to the people around me talking. They were asking each other, "what are we supposed to do?" While we are on this point. You should volunteer to be in as many shows as possible. Only by experiencing it can you relate to what your "Stars" are feeling. In chapter one we talked about how to get your people on stage. I am sure many of you will choose to ask for volunteers and have them rush the stage. I have already expressed my misgivings about the safety and other drawbacks of this technique. Whatever your method, do it quickly. Your people are seated and your first job make them feel comfortable. If a lady is wearing a skirt, have your assistant cover her so she is not exposing herself to the audience. Have them get rid of their chewing gum. There are many ways to get laughs doing this as you can see in my videos. Tell them what you are going to do and what they can expect to experience. All of this can be seen in the videos. Your induction should not be more than three minutes. Shorter than three minutes is not believable and longer than three minutes is boring. Yes, I know you have learned instant or rapid inductions, but to a novice audience member that is just not believable. Pick your stars, send the others back while explaining that it is not their fault they did not go under and invite them to try again sometime. I USE THIS LINE. "If we did not keep you on stage, it does not mean that you can't be hypnotized. It simply means, tonight you had something else on your mind.... a sound around you may have disturbed you or you could have been trying too hard. It could be any number of things...Please do try it again because 100% of all people can in fact experience hypnosis." Now it is time for you to go to work.

PACING YOUR SHOW - Your first bit is always a group skit. In your arsenal of routines, you should have at least 3 opening bits for those places such as fairs where you must do 2 or 3 shows a day and you don't want to repeat yourself. The not repeating yourself advice mainly applies to the first routine you do. Why? Because when a member of the audience sees you BEGIN the show with the same routine, they will make up their mind that they have seen the show before and walk away. It does not matter if your next 10 bits are different, they have made up their mind. I learned this the hard way when a fair manager told me he had heard from several people that my shows were all the same. The ONLY thing I did every show was the opener. I changed that and never had the complaint again. The opening bit is a group skit so you can see who your best and most animated people are. Throughout the show you should mix group and individual skits with the emphasis on the individual skits. Why? Usually when you do group skits you are creating chaos on stage. The audience does not know what to watch and will end up just watching their friends and if they don't know anyone one on stage will lose interest. Think again of yourself as the director of a great movie. If all the scenes you shoot are wide panoramic or action scenes, the movie quickly becomes boring. Group skits are most effective when you are able to feature an individual person as the skit progresses. A very good example of this in this can be seen in Michelle VanRee's Chinese rapper's routine. It is a group skit, yet she features one star at a time. Keep your movie exciting. Your next bit is an individual and is done with the person you have determined to be your best star. IF YOU MAKE A MISTAKE HERE AND THE

FIRST BIT DOES NOT WORK...THE SHOW IS OVER. Why? Everyone on stage is thinking that they are not hypnotized and if you let your first bit fail, you have reinforced that thought and nothing going forward is going to work. I wish I could say that I no longer make that mistake, but I do. Fortunately, I have learned how to recover from it but that is a lesson for another day. You won't misjudge and make the opening mistake if you pay attention. When the first bit works perfectly, it has the effect of reassuring all your stars and when they hear the applause that first person gets, they are anxious to get their own round of applause. The first individual bit should be a simple can't fail routine. Now, follow that with another "can't fail" individual bit with your worst subject. When that one works, the rest of the show is a piece of cake. Why did I suggest using your worst subject? Because when you turn him (it is usually a guy), he will become one of your best stars. A good example of a can't fail bit and the one I use most often is feet stuck. When this bit is done properly,
it cannot fail. At this point do a SIMPLE group skit such as mean teacher or speaking a different language. Keep the routine short and ALWAYS GET APPLAUSE FOR YOUR STARS. Now back to individual skits and this one should be a running gag that will repeat throughout the show. I like to use the celebrity standing and waving to

his fans when he hears applause because it trains the audience to applaud and lets them be part of the action. Also, whenever you ask for applause for the rest of the show, there is the added benefit of laughter when the person stands and waves to their fans. Please notice here how simple the bit is and how little the person has to do in order to achieve a maximum effect. They have to stand up and wave. Audience members will talk about that simple act for days. You should do two individual skits for each group skit you do. This is of course a good rule of thumb and will vary from show to show. I would guess 90% of the hypnotist performing today do almost all group skits because those are the easier skits to make work, but they do not make for the best show. If you are looking for the easy way to do this, you have chosen the wrong profession because every single time you walk on stage you are putting your reputation and skill on the line. You should be afraid of failure because IT IS THAT FEAR OF FAILURE THAT WILL MAKE YOU GOOD.

 Frantic and loud does not equate to enthusiasm. You are the hypnotist. You are the cool guy or lady. You should exude confidence. How do you do that if you are not confident? Well, dumb ass you are a hypnotist. Use it on yourself. My first show was at a night club in

Macon Georgia where I was booked to do two shows. The first show I was so frightened I think the audience could hear my knees knocking and see the sweat dripping in my eyes. I was able to do 35 minutes and it was awful. I got a smattering of polite sympathetic applause. I went downstairs to the closet I had for a dressing room to hide. It was all I could do to hold back the tears. That is when my wife came in and said, "Terry, you dumb ass, you have got to be the stupidest son of a bitch I know. You use hypnosis every day to help people with their confidence and you are too stupid to use it on yourself!" She was right! I sat down and used self-hypnosis and gave myself the suggestion that anytime I touched a microphone. I would have all the confidence, poise and charm of Dean Martin. I went back for my second show and got a standing ovation. I think it was not so much because I was so good but because of the tremendous improvement and because I had the courage to try again. If she had given me sympathy, we would have both stayed in that closet crying. To this day, when I touch a microphone, in my mind, I see Deano wearing his tux, holding a martini and charming everyone in the audience. If you believe in what you are doing.... use it!

ATTITUDE - What you should be working on now in addition to the basics we have covered is attitude. Not cocky but confident. **Never brag, let others do that for you.** This is the thing I see in so many performers today that irritates me the most. When you become "good", others will talk about it. When you brag on yourself, you are demonstrating your lack of class and humility. I have never once heard Anthony Cools or Mark Yuzuik or Mark Savard or even the late Reveen brag about how great they are. They don't need to....others do it for them.

Try in your next few shows to implement these ideas and do more individual skits. You will notice how much better the audience responds to you and your show. I encourage you to write to me or ask questions on the Facebook site.

CHAPTER THREE

THE BEST KEPT SECRET IN THE BUSINESS

Let me ask you a few questions and I would like you to answer them to yourself before moving on.

1. Is the hypnotic suggestion any more or less real if you give it through the microphone or whispered off-mic?

2. Who are the stars of the show, you or your volunteers?

3. Who do you want to make look clever?

4. Who is responsible for the wit and comedy?

Let us answer the last one first. It is up to you to come up with the funny lines and quips just as it is the movie writer's job to come up with the script. The actors or stars deliver the lines and appear to be brilliant or sensitive or brave or whatever the situation calls for. Sometimes, though rarely, one of your volunteers will come up with a funny line or response but if you allow the success of your show to depend on them, you will have a long wait. It is not their job. You need to be able to feed them the lines OFF MIC. It should appear that the cleverness was theirs and you are as surprised and amused as the audience. I know that at this point, some of you are protesting loudly saying, "that is cheating". Back to question one. Is the hypnosis more real because you give the suggestion through the microphone? Absolutely not, but it is funnier if it appears to the audience as if one of their own came up with the line or action. It is called "off Mic queuing" and here are some really some easy ones to do. When I do the missing number and have the young girl count 11 fingers...that gets a pretty good laugh, but what really makes it funny is what happens next. I say to her, you better go sit down and think about that. I put my hand on her shoulder and start to walk her back to her chair. When our backs are to the audience and the microphone is by my side, I say to her, in a voice only she can hear, "I wonder how many toes you have. You should take off your shoes and check". I then move on and start to do something with someone else. After a few seconds, I look back and act astounded that she has taken her shoes off and is counting her toes. The audience erupts with laughter. I go back and ask her how many toes. After she answers, I knock out the guy next to her and quietly say off Mic, "I wonder how many fingers he has." When she starts to count his fingers, again the audience rolls. It appears that she very naturally wondered about her toes or if anybody else had 11 fingers. She was the clever one. She was the star. The audience does not need to know how it came to be. I eventually have her removing

other people's shoes and counting their toes. With a little OFF MIC queuing, you have transformed a cute throw away bit into a hilarious "A" routine. It was changed from a 40 second bit to a running gag that can go as far as you want to take it. Almost every routine you are doing now can be enhanced this way. Why is this such a well-kept secret. I promise you every person in the business who has not mastered this technique will criticize you and say yea, but their stuff is real. That is just a way of justifying why their show is not as funny as yours. The hypnosis is just as real, you have just chosen to be an entertainer. Practice talking just loud enough for the person next to you to hear without moving your lips. Incidentally, This is one of the main reasons you should use a hand-held mic instead of a headset. You will note I keep coming back to this next thing over and over. I do that hoping that eventually you will believe me and try what I am telling you so you can see for yourself how much more effective it is. I am talking about group as opposed to individual skits. You can do off mic queuing with group skits but it is difficult to continue to expand on them. Using the technique, I just explained, you can expand an individual skit to encompass the entire group. I used to do a Jerry Springer routine (my son changed it to Trailer Park Terry which I think is much funnier). I would go by and ask each person why they were on the show. Without off mic queuing the response was usually "I'm not sure". With off Mic queuing, When I ask, "why are you here?" and move the mic to them, I say something like, "Looking for my baby daddy" or "because I like midgets" in a very low voice that only they hear. Now that I have given them a premise to work with, they will usually expand on it and come up with some pretty funny stuff. If you leave it totally up to them, they will draw a blank and the bit flops. So, if you are going to do something like that, you should already have in mind what queue you can give them.

Should you leave everyone else on stage "asleep" while you are working with one person? Absolutely Not!!! Most hypnotist do it and I have never understood why. Let me explain. Have you ever been in a hypnosis show as a volunteer (if not, that should be the next thing on your list to do)? As you know, the people hear what is going on and THEY WANT TO OPEN THEIR EYES TO WATCH. There is absolutely no reason not to let them do that and there are many reasons why you want them to be watching everyone else. One reason is simply that keeping your eyes closed for a full hour is uncomfortable. They want to look and when someone opens their eyes to look, and they will, to the audience it looks like they are faking it. The main reason I keep them all "up" until I want to do something with them is because when they watch someone else, they think, "I would have done it better or different". YOU WANT THEM COMPETING WITH EACH OTHER FOR STAR SATUS. Let them be the stars they want to be and not just a limp body. Trust me...Off Mic queuing will make the difference between just an OK show and a great show if you learn to use it properly.

WRITING MATERIAL - The biggest mistake I see most stage hypnotist making is this; they have a set skit list and they are going to do it come hell or high water. If the audience thinks the road they are going down sucks; if the audience can not relate to the material they are doing; If the volunteers are not responding to the skits....it does not matter. They have their skit list and by-god they are going to use it. In many cases this mistake is made because the hypnotist has just memorized some lines and really has no idea about how and why a hypnosis show works. This person maybe can be helped but I have neither the time or patience to try. I find more often than not the reason for this mistake is simply because they do not have enough material to pivot and change direction mid show. When I first started doing a comedy hypnosis show, I was a complete newbie. The only experience I had on stage was assisting "Mr. Hypnosis", Jack Berry and I had zero experience writing new material. To get Jack to train me I had promised to try to always do original material. He had told me I could use his material for only the first month and after that I was on my own. At the time, there were no courses or books such as this one to offer guidance. Sadly today, most hypnosis shows are copies of copies. To many hypnotist today, creating new and fresh material entails going to see someone's show and stealing what you can. In hypnosis, they do not call it stealing...it is research. Material that you copy or steal from someone else can never be your own and therefore the show can never really be yours. In this book I will be providing you with ideas for skits that I have written over the last 40 years. You are welcome to use these skits as a basis for creating your own show, but I want you really step out from the crowd and decide that you are going to have your own show and it is going to be yours because you create the content. No one ever told me how to do this but in order to keep my promise to Jack, I had to try. **Eventually, <u>I had to learn</u>**

that writing solid material is not just about stringing together skits for the sake of a laugh. It is about creating a concept that when shared, evokes emotion in the form of laughter. To write your first bit, come up with a concept based around your own personal experiences or observations. This could be something as simple as your insecurities at the gym or a smelly person sitting next to you on a bus. If the thought genuinely makes you laugh it is worth trying to make a bit out of. The talking teddy bear routine that so many people are doing is the result of watching my 2-year-old daughter play with her Teddy Ruxspin talking teddy bear. Her other favorite toy was a doll that wet. Both made her laugh and made me laugh. So, What I wanted to happen was to have an adult conversing with a stuffed animal and then have that animal pee or poop in their lap. So How do I get all this to happen. Well one way is just to tell them they will talk to the bear and then it will pee on them. I actually tried that and it got a few chuckles. What was missing was drawing the audience into the story. So, I tried it this way. The person is out and I have my assistant put the bear on the chair next to them. I say to the audience, "how many of you remember that special teddy bear or stuffed animal you had as a kid. The one that you took everywhere and was your best friend. I remember mine." Then to the subject I say, "upon awakening you will notice a new addition to our stage. Directly to your right is the cutest little teddy bear you have ever seen. You immediately love this little bear. When you look away, you will hear the little bear say, psst....I wanna talk to you...I go on and tell them that the little bear wants to be their bear and warns of the mean lady coming by later to try to throw him away. It gets a few laughs when the person seems to be talking to the bear, but when the assistant comes by to throw him away and they boldly save the bear, the laughs build. Now I explain that they can keep the bear but must keep it in their lap because I have limited seating. Do you see how I am logically building up where I want this bit to go? Next, I put them out and tell them that whenever I do a certain thing, the little bear will have an accident in their lap. When it happens, the assistant offers a napkin for them to clean up the mess. Now I have a running gag for the whole show. Let's look at how this developed. I decided what outcome I wanted...what I wanted to happen. I brought the audience into the story. I set up just the idea of talking to the bear and the surprise element of the accident. This seems so simple but I tried it at least 20 different ways to get the result I wanted. When you are first trying a bit, don't over think it. If it makes you laugh, run with it. Don't convince yourself that something is stupid or not funny enough. Some of the best bits you will ever create come from seemingly insignificant thoughts and develop into brilliant routines over time. Whenever I hear a joke that makes me laugh, I try to think of ways to make that happen in a hypnosis show. The routine where I have the guy sing happy birthday to be able to remember his name came from a stupid joke my wife told me. The Jerry Springer show made me laugh so I turned it into a routine. Where's the beef made me laugh...it became a bit. Ask yourself, what makes you laugh. That, dear reader is the starting point. Use what makes you laugh. Whenever possible it is good to share with the audience where the idea comes from...the thought process that sparked the idea for what they are about to see. This brings the audience more into your world and lets them be a bigger part of the show.

LOOK AT THINGS WITH NEW EYES - Several years ago, I started doing something in my show that forced me to be creative and write new material on the spot. I told my assistant to hand me some item in the middle of the show. It could be anything as long as I had no idea what it was going to be before the show. If I could not think of a skit to do with the item she gave me, I would pay her a $50 bonus for the night. You only have to lose 50 bucks a couple of times before you learn to be creative. The secret to creating something on the spot was to view the item with new eyes. I would imagine that I had no idea what the item was or what it was used for and like an anthropologist I would try to figure out a use for the item from just looking at it. A tin can might be ancient idol or a part for my car. A rope might be a hair piece or a magic wand. A fly swatter might be a musical instrument. The idea was to imagine it to be something that it obviously is not. Most times I would explain to the audience what was going on and that would really put me on the spot. By the way, this is a good idea just in case the bit flops because you can say, " I did not say it would be good...I said I would use it", which gets a small sympathy laugh. Most times however the bit is funny and really appreciated by the audience. Occasionally it will be a gem that you will add to your regular repertoire. The main thing to remember is if you have a mop...don't tell them to mop the floor. That is just not funny. Dancing with the mop is funny. Try this.... Go to a dollar store and buy $20 dollars' worth of goofy items. Don't try to figure out what you are going to do with them. Take them home and spread them out on a table and just sit back and look at them. Pick up any item and play with it. Make it talk to you. Ask it what it does. Within a few minutes, ideas will start to pop into your head. Write them down. After you have several ideas start to combine them. The wilder the better. This is where you will find the magic start to happen and although I can't explain it, it never fails. An idea will suddenly crystalize and it will make you laugh. Now go back to rule one...if it makes you laugh, use it. To begin with you will try 6 or 7 ideas to get one "keeper", but as you get better at it you will be keeping 1 out of 3.

PUT TOGETHER A THINK TANK - Have you ever noticed that when you are sitting around chatting with friends and cracking jokes you get really creative? Someone tells a joke or story and that reminds you of another joke or story. Use this to create material.... create a think tank. The ideal person to do this with is someone who likes and has an interest in your show and your success. A spouse, an assistant, other performers are all good people to invite to your think tank. The rules of a think tank are simple. There can be NO NEGATIVITY. The more outlandish the idea the better. Nothing is taboo. Now start tossing out ideas. One stupid crack will give the idea for another stupid idea and while you are laughing at that, a workable bit develops. Other ideas combine with that and you tame it down some to make it acceptable to an audience and before long you have created a complete routine. I have come up with as many as 20 workable totally original bits in a 1 hour think tank meeting. You can start with something you have seen before and try to make it funnier and as every person adds something, the routine takes on a life of its own and seems to create itself. Your very best material will come from a think tank and collaboration. If you do this just once a week, within a month you will have enough material for 2 more completely different shows. You should have enough material so that you can appeal to and adapt to any audience. When the response to a particular bit is not what you wanted or expected or if the audience seems bored or antsy you can immediately switch to a new concept. I am guessing you are probably a lot smarter than me so you may get faster results. I generally have to try a bit 4 or 5 different ways to find a way that works the way I want it to. Sometimes it begins as a group skit and after several tries, I do the bit with just 1 or 2 people. Sometimes what I thought was going to be an individual bit develops into a group skit. More times than I can count, the bit I thought was going to be great gives me an idea that turns out to be really great. The rule is....be flexible. Just because you originally imagine a routine one way does not mean that is the way it is going to develop. Creativity comes when you allow the bits to grow and develop naturally. When it comes down to it, the only way to get really good at writing material is to consistently work at it every single day so get started.

CHAPTER FOUR

YOUR INDUCTION

A few months ago, I was working with a hypnotist on improving his show. It was a few minutes before showtime and I saw him sitting in the audience focusing hard on a wad of papers and notes in his hands. I walked over and inquired what he was doing. He replied, "I am studying your induction." I asked why. He told me he wanted to be able to get the same high percentage of people under that I do, so he was studying how I phrased each line. My head exploded because we had spent the entire morning talking about how it did not matter WHAT you said. It is the authority with which you say it. My first inclination was to ask if he had not heard ANYTHING or learned ANYTHING. Why was I wasting my time? Before I spoke, I remembered why...I was being paid a lot of money which I had no desire to give back. Instead of berating him I said, Sam (not his real name) put away all of that stuff and watch this show. Pay particular attention to the induction. The show began and I got my volunteers on stage and I began the induction. It went something like this. Everyone, as I speak to you over the next few minutes the sound of the Buffalo behind you will not disturb you in any way. You will just to continue to relax. Should you see a duck walk across the stage it will not alarm or surprise you but relax you even more. Now as you find your eyes growing tired your feet feel like turnips and this will cause you to want to close the eyes. That's the way...show those turnips who is boss. I continued in this vain for two minutes saying the most ridiculous and outrageous things. Whatever popped into my mind I said...with authority? At one point I think I actually said, if the person next to you has gas, the aroma will relax you even more. I got 7 out of 8 under. I probably would have gotten 8 had I not mentioned the farts. I looked at my student and his jaw was in his lap. There are no magic words of phrases. Hypnosis is based on belief and trust in you as the hypnotist. The people on stage with you assume you know what you are doing, ergo if you do it....it must be right. I use the same basic induction that I have used for dozens of years, not because the words are magic but because I am comfortable with them and can SPEAK THEM WITH AUTHORITY! That is why it is so very important that your reputation precede you. You never want to be a "surprise" guest. The induction is there to make it believable. Street hypnosis is a perfect example of how "what" you say does not matter. Speaking of street hypnosis, I would like to take a moment to talk about that. Although it requires a great deal of skill, I am not a fan. To me, it looks like someone showing off. Now before you get your panties in a bunch let me explain. For years if you wanted to see a hypnosis show, you had to wait and anticipate. When you finally got the opportunity...it was special. Now there is nothing to anticipate, go to any local bar or pub and there he is...THE HYPNOTIST...working at the tables and not on stage. I don't question the skill or training required to pull it off, it is just that personally I do not like the optics. When every guy in the bar had a thumb tip in his pocket to impress the ladies it puts a bad taste in people's mouth about the uniqueness and entertainment value of a magic show. The people standing around enjoy it but hey, that is Tom the insurance guy. I personally really like the non-induction induction used by street hypnotist and use it often...when the situation requires. Grad nights are a perfect place to use that induction because there, more than any place else, it does not matter WHAT you say. At my theatre here in Florida, the hotel has a large pool that is always packed with people. They decided to have a movie night and asked if I could provide a half-hour entertainment before the movie to get the people out of the pool and in a receptive mood for the movie. They wanted 1/2 hour to get the people's attention. This is the perfect place to use a non-induction induction. I have 10 people standing in front of 4 chairs. I have them place their feet shoulder width for stability and ask them to close their eyes and imagine what it would feel like if their eyes were stuck together. I repeat, "imagine the eyes are stuck several times. Now in a moment when you try to open your eyes, you will find that they are actually stuck. Imagine they are stuck tight as you try to open them now. You will find they are in fact stuck tight. Try now. They are in fact stuck!" now as a few of them open their eyes, I simply motion for them to go back to their lounge chair. Inevitability, there will be 4 or 5 people who will struggle to open the eyes. I tap their forehead, tell them to open their eyes and take a seat. DONE! This technique takes about 40 seconds. Now I have them seated and go to the person who had the most trouble opening their eyes and put them out with a pressure/release hand movement. Now the show has started and I have 27 minutes left to do comedy material. In this situation, street hypnosis works. It grabs attention quickly and then moves to a stage (or pool deck in this case). It happens so fast that people who thought they would not like a hypnosis show were drawn in before they had time to think about it. Now, I do not like using this technique on stage because over the years people have been conditioned to believe that it takes several minutes to induce hypnosis and I am not there to challenge their beliefs. For a theatre, the relaxation induction is more believable...and to me that is what I am comfortable with so it works. If you are comfortable with having people stick their finger in their nose and push the sleep button, that will work for you.

CHAPTER FIVE

SHOW BUSINESS IS TWO WORDS

When I was starting my career, I was fortunate enough to meet two gentlemen who became instrumental in shaping and directing my performances so that I could eventually become one of the most successful stage hypnotists in the business. One of those gentlemen was Jay Finlay who I talk about extensively in the video KEY TO INTEGRITY. The other gentleman was Jay's boss at Main Track Entertainment Agency, Bob Vincent. In addition to being an accomplished performer, Bob had also been entertainment Director for Bill Harrah at Harrah' casino in Reno. Bob's knowledge of show business is still unequaled. In Bob's bestselling book, "Show Business is Two Words", Bob offered incredible insight into this business of ours. In addition to being my friend, Bob became my manager. With permission from his widow Cindy Vincent, I submit the following excerpts from one of Bob's books for your consideration.

FROM SHOW BUSINESS IS TWO WORDS *There is no doubt that sex between two consenting adults can be exhilarating, but intercourse between an audience and a performer, including three of four climaxes, is just as satisfying an experience to a hungry performer, and the exhilaration and headiness is just as satisfying to the audience. If you do not bring each audience to a climax at least one or twice during each show, you have only "diddled" them, and left them with an unsatisfied feeling. As a result, you have not fulfilled the real reason you were on stage. I relate the satisfying of the audience to sexual intercourse because both relationships must be tender, very thorough, and totally satisfying to both parties. To achieve this, you must be in a "one on one" relationship with each member of the audience from the moment you walk on stage until you leave. I can assure you that without consistent personal contact with your audience, you will never become a true solid performer. This does not mean that you cannot reach some degree of success without it because there are many*

artists who get a hit record or sudden unplanned exposure. The only way to continue your stardom is to become a consistently solid performer. With this book, I cannot promise to make you a star, but by studying the materials, I can give you the tools with which you can become a "solid" performer. You see, there is a fine line between giving a plastic, well-rehearsed performance to a sea of faceless people and an honest "one on one" personal relationship between you and each witness to your performance. The amateur performer tends to show how clever he or she is, and gives what I call a plastic, contrived performance. If your attitude on stage is to attempt to show the audience how clever you are, or how handsome or pretty you are, and that they are lucky you showed up...this is a fatal mistake.

YOU MUST BE HONEST IN YOUR LOVE FOR THE AUDIENCE, love of your profession; and your only purpose for being onstage is to give them a thoroughly moving experience that they will remember. Remember, were it not for these people, you would have a 9 to 5 job? They provide you with not only the material things you might have but the opportunity to do what you love.

Once onstage you must totally forget your identity. You cannot be concerned with your "ego-self" and still give the audience the performance they deserve. In other words, once you are on the stage you should not be concerned with how your hair looks, or how your suit or dress fits. You should be unconcerned about your physical self and be involve with a spiritual, intangible connection with the audience. Only in this way can you really connect and know what the audience needs.

The audience must be taken through a variety of emotional experiences in order to be completely satisfied. You must pace your show so that it affects them in many different ways. Just like with a singer, too *many fast songs are not good and too many slow songs are not good. If you give too much of any one thing for too long, you will lose the audience. You must instinctively feel your audience to know when you have reached that certain point where a change is due. Young inexperienced performers have not developed this fine instinct and as a result, they keep losing their audiences. A real pro rarely loses an audience once he gets them. In most cases, the real pro gets his audience in the first minute he or she is on stage and they keep the audience until the curtain drops.*

Establish your image and keep it. Each performer, whether they recognize it or not has a certain image in the minds of the public. Once you create that image, you must never destroy it. Jack Benny was stingy. Dean Martin Drank. Frank Sinatra was the coolest guy in town. True or not, you must never show the public that you have feet of clay. The public does not like to have their idols changed in any way.

Keep Your Act Fresh. There is nothing worse for an artist than to get bored with his own material. It does not matter how good an act you have, after you have done the exact same act for years, you will find the original "thrill" is gone. The same is true when you are doing someone else's material. There is no thrill. Your boredom is transmitted to your audience. We have all seen performers phoning it in. You cannot fake enthusiasm when you don't honestly feel it.

You must stay on top of the changing trends in show business. Many artists have died fighting the change in the public's taste, and not keeping up with the changing trends. You must stay abreast with what is happening. You cannot assume that because you were a success yesterday, you will enjoy the same success tomorrow. This is the very reason I do not talk about the crowds of thousands I have performed for or the many television shows I have appeared on. I was told once by someone who knew, and I believe it to be true, "You are only as good as your last show." The public is fickle and will drop you just as quickly as they accepted you. Plan on how good you are going to be tomorrow because no one is interested in how good you were yesterday. This is a sad fact of our business...learn to accept it and you will be miles ahead in the game.

Maintain a warm, 'arm's length" friendship with all of the people you work with. You must always remember success is a two-way street and if you have been a jerk while you were hot, when you begin to "slide", they will all help speed your demise! Remember, nothing is guaranteed forever in our business. THANKS BOB!

Show Business Is Two Words, SHOW and BUSINESS!!! This is the one I wish I had paid more attention to. I have made millions of dollars and I spent it like it was never going to end. It did. If you are the least bit bright, and if you are smart enough to know that your success is really temporary, you will hire and listen to a competent business manager and also a smart show showbiz attorney. They are invaluable to you. They may be expensive, but at the peak of your earning power their service fee can be written off. Pay attention to your business but do not try to run it yourself. Your focus should be on becoming the best performer you can be and hire someone else to do the things you are not good at. There are many people in our business who try to do the marketing, web work, promotion, booking and performing. Do what you do best and let someone else do what they do best. Doing it this way, I promise, there will be a bigger pie to split.

MORE FROM BOB VINCENT
 In 1979, I purchased and read Bob Vincent's book, "Show Business Is Two Words". To be perfectly honest, I only purchased the book because I was mentioned in

the book as an up and coming star. Like most of you, I did not know what I did not know and assumed because I had done a few successful shows I already knew it all. Boy, was I wrong? Recently while re-reading this book, I found some additional gems I had missed on previous readings. There was a chapter on pacing your show that I had ignored because it was speaking primarily to singers. At the time, I thought that my area of entertainment was different and those golden rules did not apply. Now, with 50 years' experience, I realize that had I listened to Bob's advice in 1979, I could have saved myself 35 years of trial and error to arrive at the same facts that were laid out for me so many years ago. Entertainment is entertainment and whether you use songs, jokes, juggling or hypnosis, the principles are the same. I will present here that chapter. If while reading it, you decide that because he is talking to singers it does not apply to you, read it again. I assure you that every principle applies. I really want you to THINK about how the rules relate to your own area of show business.

For the moment, let's think back to your purpose for being on stage. The audience must be satisfied, or you have failed. It's just common sense that in order for you to make your job easier, you must create a good impression on the audience immediately, because you are actually being auditioned by them each and every show. You cannot assume that because you killed them on the last show, you are going to be a guaranteed success thereafter. I am sure you have heard performers say, "Boy, that was a lousy audience.!" In truth it was not a lousy audience, the performer did a lousy show. Please remember, "there are no bad songs, only bad singers." knowing that your first impression is going to be lasting, and that you must immediately convince the audience that they are going to get their money's worth, it is wise that your opening number, or "chunk" as I call it, must do a multitude of things for you. Chunks are not bits or routines but rather segments of the show such as opener or pre-talk. It must:

• Establish your humility and sincerity.

• Establish your credibility as a singer, dancer, musician, comic, etc.

• Establish your intelligence in putting together a clever opener, which is relative to the taste of your audience.

• Establish your personal identity so they will remember you.

• Give them bits and pieces of what they will be seeing and hearing for the balance of the show.

- Make them realize you have a good sense of pacing, so they won't become bored with too much similarity of material.

- Establish you have class. In other words, your opening chunk should be almost like an overture. It should start with an exciting intro and first song, and without playing or singing full choruses of any one song, the opener should continue on with a direct segue out of one song into another, and so on, with changes of tempo and changes of keys. Of course, the end of the opening chunk should build to an exciting climax, with an obvious, clearly designed finish, so there is no doubt in the audience's mind that they should "get ready to applaud!" After the opening "Chunk", without saying a word, you should go into your second song, which should have a totally different feel. After the second song, you should have created desire in the audience's mind to want to get to know you better so now is the time to talk to them and say "Hello, I'm John Jones and I'm here to show you a good time." Here is where you should have something humorous to say, not a joke necessarily, but something to establish you as a human being with human frailties the same as your audience. Thanks again Bob, I never stop learning from you!

Take a moment now and go back over Bob's formula and see how you can relate it to your own show. keep in mind, this is a formula, not a script. The material will change but the feel that the material you choose gives the audience will not change. The material will change because each audience is different. Comparing your show to a football team, you can imagine what would happen to the team if the quarterback wrote out a list of consecutive plays the night before the game, and called the plays exactly is he wrote them out regardless of what the opponents defense was doing? Don't assume that you will have the same kind of audience each show. It never happens. I know several artists who have a set script, with the same order of skits and the same patter and conversation between each bit. The only way that they can continue in this business is if they have a new audience each time they walk on stage. If you can work as an act in the main room in Las Vegas, you might get away with the Pat act, but there is still one big danger under those circumstances. After a time, you get bored with your own act. This is when you lose your "one on one contact" with the audience! Most all of the big super stars work to a new audience every show, but still vary their material just so that this separation from the audience does not happen. There is nothing that will kill you quicker than being an exact copy of a currently established star. Nobody wants to buy an imitation of what they already have. One of the big dangers in our business is mediocrity. In the beginning of your career, when you realized that you are not well-equipped, you worked hard because you knew that you must get some measure of success just to hold onto a job. After you have some measure of success is the most dangerous part of your entire show business career. At this point many an artist withers and dies. Because you were fairly successful, and because you were being paid fairly regularly, you have a tendency to relax and "dog it". I'm warning you that this is the crucial moment. It is vitally important that you recognize the danger signs, and keep on working on your act and your skills, so that you can get over the hump of mediocrity. There is no such thing as "that's good enough". Many, many established stars have made the mistake of thinking that their popularity would last forever. They didn't continue to progress and stay up with the times, and for that reason, they are no longer in demand. In our business there is no such word as "forever" or "never". How many times have you heard someone say "he'll never make it or he'll last forever"? The people that said those things have had to eat their words. With the ever-changing taste of the masses everything is possible! In order for you to be a great performer, it is necessary that you maintain a fresh act at all times. I don't care how great an act you start with. If you don't constantly add new material and new bits to it, what started out to be great has got to slowly become uninteresting. It isn't that the original material becomes less effective, it's only that you yourself become bored with it. I don't care how good the story is, or how great the song is, the more you tell the story, or sing the song, or do the bit the less effective it becomes in terms of moving you. As a result, when your own act doesn't move you, it naturally no longer moves your audience. I am certain that you can think back to the times when you added a brand-new piece of material to your act, how exciting it was for you the first time you did it for an audience. When it no longer works for you, it isn't because it is no longer good, it's just that you no longer deliver it with your original enthusiasm. It again comes down to honesty. You can't be honest with material you no longer believe in. If this happens to you it's time to add some new material. This is a constant need so you should never rest on your laurels. Keep looking and adding new material to your act constantly. It may be more work for you, but you'll be far more successful on stage. Each show that you do should be considered as a brand-new separate entity and a new challenge. Just because you killed them on your last show doesn't mean that you will kill them on your next show. You must remember that each time you step on stage in front of an audience, there is always a certain amount of auditioning going on. You have to reprove yourself to the audience, even though some of the same people are still there from the last show. You must remember that they have spent additional money for food and beverage, and they again must get their money's worth from you. I'm going to pose a hypothetical example for you which will illustrate the point. If you were told and believed that the job you were on is the only job left in the world for you, and that you have to please each member of the audience thoroughly or be taken outside and shot! What kind of show would you do? The trouble with many performers is that they don't make total commitment to every show, because they assume that if they don't do well on this job, that will always be another one. If you truly believed that the job you were on is the only job in the world for you, your whole attitude would change. Believe me when I tell you, you do not have an alternative, this is your only job, take good care of it or it could be your last.

CHAPTER SIX

BE READY

I have been in show business for 50 plus years and many of the lesson I have learned came from other entertainers, some of them major stars and some just struggling like me. The lessons I learned had been told to me before or I had heard them from my agents and friends but until I actually saw them at work, they did not hit home. In this chapter, I would like to share some personal stories that have taught me valuable lessons. I hope they hit home with you as much as they did me.

BE READY FOR ANYTHING The Heebie Jeebies are an extremely talented a cappella group that I have worked with many times. They are constantly rehearsing and every time I see them, they are even better than the time before. Over the years we began playing practical jokes on each other during performances. The jokes were always fun and funny and made us prove our professionalism on stage. The following example is one of many gags that have happened over the years. A simple and fun gag is to place a television inside one of the stages monitors so that only the act can see it. When the show starts, you start playing a porno film that only they can see. I did that to The Heebie Jeebies at the Calgary Stampede one year and the guys instantly created a routine where they could take turns standing in front of the monitor showing the porno film. They never missed a beat so I was determined to try again. The next day, I got the sound man to play one of their recordings through the main sound system --- A song different than the one they were singing. As they started to sing, a different song was coming out of the speakers. Again, they did not miss a beat, they switched to the song we were playing and the audience had no idea anything had happened.

ROLL WITH THE FLOW - Working with THE DIAMONDS was fun not only because I had grown up listening to their music and they were so professional, but as it turns out they were all really nice guys. When The Diamonds took the stage they would always begin with "Little Darlin" one of their many mega hits. The crowd would always burst into thunderous applause and cheers when they began the song. One year my show was on right before theirs and I made a pact with the crowd. The band members were all down in their dressing rooms and could not hear as I explained practical joke day to the crowd. I asked 4500 people to not applaud or make a sound when the band started. It was show time and The Diamonds were behind the

Terry Stokes-2012

Stage Hypnotist
Terry Stokes Jr.-2016

My wife **JJ** and
daughter **TerriAnne**

My 1st assistants,
**Brandy and
ChaCha**

When I thought
I was Elvis.

Chubby Checker was such a pleasure to work with. You will notice that my "fro" was bigger than his.

Glenn Campbell had just released "Rhinestone Cowboy" and was the biggest name in country music.

Getting to meet and work with **George Burns** was one of the biggest thrills of my career.

With **Kris Kristofferson** in about 1989.

Like everyone else, I was in awe of **Brenda Lee**'s talent. In this photo I think she was standing on a box.

TG Shepard came into my show one night after his concert in Canada. He got hypnotized and I had no idea who he was. I think I made him Elvis.

Red Skelton was one of the sweetest people I have ever met. He was kind to everyone and took the time for all his fans.

Jim Nabors was the most talented performer I have ever worked with. He could do it all !

With **Helen Reddy** and I think the year was about 1986.

As an aspiring stage hypnotist you car imagine my excitement to meet The Hi Hypnotist **Pat Collins.**

Not everyone can boast about sharing a stage with **My Little Ponies!**

Since I was 18 years old I have admired and idolized this man. I am so proud to to claim **Mr. Glenn W. Turner** as a true friend. For those who do not remember Mr. Turner, I suggest you google and read his inspirational story

With the original **Righteous Brothers** at a California Fair I can not remember.

I was thrilled to meet **Kevin Costner** briefly at The Calgary Stampede.

With **Mel Tillis** right after Smokey and the Bandit was released in 1977.

In Las Vegas with one of my all time favorite film icons, **Tony Curtis.**

With **Phyllis Diller** in Hot Springs Arkansas

I am so proud of **Michelle VanRee.** She began as my assistant and evolved into one of the most accomplished female hypnotist I have known.

With **Michael Johns.** Michael is one of the funniest and most talented hypnotist I have every worked with.

Kellie Karl and I were talking about producing a new show called "Battle Of The Hypnotist". You can tell from the photo who would have won.

Amanda Alridge, was such a great stage partner. I could write another book just about her. She is my "one that got away".

the curtains listening to their introduction… there was not a sound from the audience. All the guys looked a little confused as they began to play Little Darlin and an ocean of people stared silently at them as if they were singing in a foreign language. At first, they thought the main speakers in the sound system were down, but it was soon apparent that everything was working properly. There was a pause built into the performance to allow the crowd noise to die down before they continued the song, but this time there was no crowd noise. Like the professionals that they are, they played off the silence. One of the guys said, "I guess that ain't the one they want to hear, another said maybe we should do some Elvis. At that point I came out on stage to let the crowd know the joke was over and the Diamonds got a 5-minute standing ovation before the show even started. That was one of the best concerts I have ever seen and I think part of it was because of the little joke the crowd had played on the band, the fans felt an extra connection.

KNOW YOU AUDIENCE Mark Yuziuk is a very talented stage hypnotist and one of my closest friends. Shortly after I bought my first house in Las Vegas, Mark and his girlfriend came for a visit. One afternoon they went for a walk and didn't come back for several hours. Turns out

Mark had found a house for sale down the street that had 500 more square feet than my house. He bought the damn thing. He swears he did it just so he could say he had a bigger house than me. That summer Mark had to be out of town for a month so he gave me his house keys and asked that I keep an eye on his house. While he was gone, I replaced every picture in his house with pictures of me. Photos of me. Oil paintings of me. I put 8x10's under the toilet seats. Little pictures of me inside of ever glass and on every dish. My picture on his pillow cases. My picture on milk cartons and every can in the pantry. There was a total of 500 pictures of me in his house. He said he was finding them for months. Now Mark is a clever guy and he took his time getting me back. What he did is to me, one of the most brilliant and beautiful practical jokes ever played. I was booked for a week in some little town in Nevada that I cannot even recall the name of. My assistant/ girlfriend was sick so I had to go to the date by myself. Mark had a dozen roses delivered to me at the front desk of the hotel where I was staying with an open card that read "I wuv and miss you Terry Werry. Love, your Markie Warkie". He then called the hotel and in his gayest voice, explained that he was my lover. He explained that I was just coming out of the closet and was still uncomfortable and might even deny our love. It turns out the desk clerk was also gay and promised Mark his full support. Mark had given the same story to the florist and within a matter of hours I had the support of the entire gay community of this little town. Not only was I forced to be gay for a week (I remained abstinent because I was loyal to Mark) but I had a great opening night. The gay community was there every night to support me. They were all really fantastic folks.

Red Skelton - Remember where you came from and know where you are going. One of the saddest things about this business of ours is how it can make you forget your roots. It happens before you realize it. With thousands of people applauding your every word and telling you how great you are, it is very easy to get lost and start believing the BS. It was starting to happen to me when I had the opportunity to meet and work with Red Skelton. Mr Skelton was as humble as he was talented. The lesson I learned from him saved me the heartbreak of the crushing reality that I was not special. I grew up watching Red Skelton and could not believe my good fortune when I was given the opportunity to meet and work with him. It was in Yakima Washington and we were both performing at the Washington State Fair. There was a rehearsal scheduled in the ballroom of the Red Lion Motel and I was waiting impatiently in my room for the call that would put me in the same room with this legend of comedy. There was a 17-piece orchestra waiting and several members of the press were also in attendance. I received the call. Mr. Skelton had been delayed. Would I like to come and wait or would I like to have someone call me when the great man arrived. I am going to meet Red Skelton - I will come and wait. As I left my room, I noticed a crowd of people gathered outside one of the rooms down the hall. As I got closer, I discovered that the entire maid staff and maintenance crew were huddled together watching something going on in one of the rooms. It was then that I heard Mr. Skelton performing Gertrude and Heathcliff, one of his classic routines. I learned that when asked if she would be attending the show, a maid had responded to Mr. Skelton that she could not afford the ticket. He had her call her entire family and friends and gather the staff of the hotel to his room. He did his entire show for those fans - well over an hour. That moment standing in the hallway of the Red Lion, I learned one of the greatest lessons I could ever learn about this business I so loved. I saw a true star shine. Later that day I had the opportunity to spend several hours chatting with and listening to his wonderful stories about show business legends that I had only heard about. One story he told intrigued me more than any other and I will retell it here. Red Skelton told me that when he was a very young man and his movie career was just beginning to take off, he was approached by a group of business men with a proposition that almost changed his life. They were a group of Christian business men who wanted to put together a traveling revival. They would front all the money and book the tours. They wanted to create the greatest revival that had ever been - but they need a front man. They wanted a preacher that people would love and could relate to. They wanted someone to front the movement that people would trust and follow. They wanted Red Skelton to be that front man and they offered him the job. After several days of soul searching, Red Skelton decided to turn down their generous offer. The business men were disappointed but they accepted his decision and went with their second choice for the job - Billy Graham.

GEORGE BURNS - Try to weave a love story into your career Many people only remember George Burns from the "Oh God "movies, but trust me when I say he was as much a legend and talent in show business as Elvis. I got to meet Mr. Burns in Yakima Washington about one month before the first "Oh God" movie was released. My wife at the time, Brandy, was an even bigger fan of George Burns than I was. She rehearsed her greeting to him for hours on the morning we were to meet him. Hello Mr. Burns, it's so nice to meet you Mr. Burns, I am such a fan Mr. Burns. She rehearsed in the mirror. She made me listen and critique each potential greeting. Finally, she was ready. We were picked up and driven out to meet him. When he came out of his dressing trailer, Brandy rushed up to him, burst into tears and slobbered, "You're George Burns". He smiled, looked at me and said, "Is her name Gracie?" I think it was because of Brandy's greeting that Mr. Burns liked us. We were invited into his trailer where we spent several wonderful hours listening to him talk about Gracie. He mentioned his new movie almost as an afterthought and then went back to another Gracie story. We left him that afternoon knowing that the greatest love story either of us had ever heard was the story of George Burns and Gracie Allen. It turns out that George Burns liked practical Jokes too. To understand what happened you need to visualize how his stage was assembled for that evening's performance. The stage itself was almost 25 feet high. It was towed onto the field by trucks in three sections. The larger main stage where the performer and band worked and two wings for either side where the columns of speakers set and where the stairs were attached. The crew that day had reversed the right and left wings as they were towed in and dropped into place. In that configuration the wings would not fit into place and there was a 2-foot gap between the sections of stage. There was not time to move the sections so it was decided that someone would be available to escort Mr. Burns safely on and off the stage. That evening George Burns, a man in his 80's shuffled to center stage and delivered one of the most fantastic shows I have ever seen. He sang, danced, told jokes and stories and wowed the 15,000 people for well over an hour. He got two curtain calls and a standing ovation. He was supposed to exit stage left where his escort was waiting to guide him safely over the deadly crevice. He turned right and was shuffling towards the gap between stage sections. From the ground people began shouting. "Mr. Burns Stop, go back. He continued in that stooped shoulder shuffle walk for which he was famous directly towards the crevice. There were at least 20 of us on the ground screaming up for him to stop. He was at the very edge of the gap when this little 85-year-old man jumped straight up and landed on the other side of the crevice.

He turned and looked down at our stunned faces and said, "Gotcha".

Phyllis Diller Learn to laugh at yourself Phyllis Diller was a wonderful lady and as I found out a great sport. I worked with her in Hot Springs Arkansas. She was in the main showroom and I was in the smaller adjoining showroom. We had been there three days and had not yet met. My show was at 7 and Phyllis went on at 9. I was doing a bit in the show where, using hypnosis I had someone think they were Phyllis Diller. This person would sign autographs and usually do a pretty good impression of the great comedian. I was doing that bit one night when for a reason I didn't understand the crowd started cheering from the back of the room. Phyllis had been watching my show from the back and when my hypnotized Phyllis stood for the applause, the fabulous Miss Diller came up to get her own autograph. She got the autograph and then started asking my hypnotized subject about Fang, her stage character's husband. Their conversation was hysterical. That night we became friends and it is a moment on stage that I will never forget.

Exposure - A fan is a fan no matter where you find them. As an entertainer, I love to be recognized when out in public. Anyone in the business who says otherwise is lying. It does not really matter where you are, being recognized feels good. Several years ago, I was in Calgary Alberta filming a promo piece for the local television station to promote the upcoming Stampede. The work finished early so I went out for a night on the town. I returned to my hotel at about 3am and as the saying goes, I had to pee like a race horse. My room was on the 20th floor and I knew there was no way I could hold it for that long, slow elevator ride. I knew there were restrooms in the lobby so I hurriedly paid for my cab and ran inside. The men's room was at the end of a long hallway and I knew I was not going to make it. The ladies' room was about 10 steps away. It was 3 am and no one was around, so I started into the ladies' room. To make things go faster, I unzipped my pants as I began to push on the door. By the time I stepped through the door I had my taliwaker out and ready to do my business. I look up and standing by the sink is a lady washing her hands. I am standing there with my pecker in my hand. She looks at my face, then down at my crotch and back up to my face. She smiles and says, "You're Terry Stokes". It's nice to be recognized.

<u>Jay Finlay - Integrity</u> "I won't be wronged I won't be insulted I won't be laid a hand upon. I don't do these things to other people And I require the same from them ". These are the opening lines from a great western called "The Shootist" with John Wayne. I have always loved cowboy flicks because the cowboys always seemed to live by a code, A code of conduct, A code of belief and a code of morals and actions. Throughout my life, I have sought out people I admired and tried to emulate the qualities in them that I wanted to develop for myself. I suggest everyone do this because it gives you a model to follow. In my life there have been quite a few role models. There was of course my father whose tenacity and love of life was legendary. There was Glenn W. Turner whose love of his fellow man allowed him to become one of the most beloved men in America. Jack Berry was the greatest hypnotist I ever saw, and Billie Dee Cox was the greatest entertainer. I studied and tried to learn from all of these people...But I think the greatest lessons I every learned came from someone you have probably never heard of. His name was Jay Madison Finlay. From Jay, I learned many things but two stand out in my mind. Two things...first anything can be fixed with duct tape and second, I learned what it meant to be honest and have

integrity and character. Jay was the last of a breed...a man whose work ethic never faltered and whose honesty and integrity are remembered by all who knew him. To understand the man, I need to tell you his story. Jay Finlay grew up in Washington State and Alaska. As a young man, he dreamed of being a champion Olympic skier. When he was 19, his dreams were about to come true when he was selected to represent America in the winter Olympics. Like many 19-year old kids , to celebrate he decided to go drinking. He lied to his coach about where he was going and proceeded to hit the night spots of Vancouver. In the early hours of the morning, Jay crashed his car. He was in a coma for several months, and when he woke up, he realized he was lucky to be alive but his dreams of being an Olympic champion were dead. Both of his ankles had been pulverized and he was never to ski again. Jay accepted the responsibility for what had happened and made himself a promise...he would never again have a drink...and he would never again lie. I met Jay In the late 70's. My career as a stage hypnotist was about 2 months old and I still had not found an agent to represent me. I was in Orlando Florida walking past a motel room when I looked in the window and saw a man sitting at the table sorting band photos. I assumed correctly that he was an agent. I knocked on his door and a 6ft 4 in giant answered. I introduced myself and started lying right away. I told him I had the greatest hypnosis show ever and had just fired my agent. He interrupted me and said he was too busy to listen to lies so if I would excuse him, he was very busy. I went by his room the next day and ask him if I could start over...he chuckled and said go ahead. I told him I had actually only done a few shows and couldn't even get an agent to talk to me. I told him I had a job for 3 more nights at the Holiday Inn down the street and was just working for my food and room. If I didn't get an agent or another job, I didn't have enough money to get out of town. He said he would come see me that night. I didn't see him there so I assumed he had just forgotten. The next day I found he had checked out of his room so I gave up on yet another agent. Two nights later after my last show, as I was leaving the club Jay was waiting for me in the lobby. He said he had been there all three nights but didn't want me to know because he wanted to see who I was when no one was looking. I didn't understand that at the time and didn't for many years, but I never forgot it. He bought me breakfast that night and said he would be my personal agent and manager. I asked about a contract with him and he said, sure, we would draw one up. We never did. Jay let me stay at his house until he could get me some jobs and I got on my feet. Thirty years later he was still my agent and manager and we still never had a contract. In the thirty years I knew him I never knew him to lie about anything, which I learned is highly unusual for an agent. Oh, Jay could be tactful, if my girlfriend asks him if the pants made her ass look big, he might just say, no, the pants don't do it. Because Jay would not lie, he would not tolerate anyone that would. Once, in Puyluup Washington, a theatre manager promised us his room could seat 1500 people. We rented the room and sold 1500 tickets. The day of the show the manager told us that the fire department would only allow him to have 1000 people in the room and that he couldn't use his balcony. He had known this before but had lied to get the sale. He told us that if he allowed the 1500 in the room the potential fine would cause him to lose money on the event. Jay nodded his head and told the manager he wanted to show him something in the balcony. They walked off. About three minutes later I heard a noise and looked up. This 6"4" giant was dangling the theatre manager over the balcony by one ankle and in the calmest voice I have ever heard, He said, "son, you need to learn that your word is more important than your money." That night we had 1500 people at the show. By this time, I was Jay's only client and he was more of my business partner than my agent. We were the first show to begin videotaping and selling the tapes.... his idea. We were the first show to sell the smoking and weight tapes...his idea. We were the first to move into the fair industry...his idea. It was Jay's code not to tolerate dishonesty in any way. He knew there were thieves in our business, but we did not have to associate or do business with them. If the bank made an error in his favor, he would take them their money back. Jay would tell me if a person will steal little things, then they will steal big ones. He told me that one of the reasons he had decided to represent me was I had told him I would not do anyone else's material...it was stealing.

Jay smoked for 40 years and two years after he quit smoking, he got throat cancer. They removed his voice box and teeth and started him on chemo therapy. We bought a gold mine in Arizona and Jay moved there and started digging gold. He let his beard grow and I swear he looked like Gabby Hayes. Some of you younger folks don't know who that is, but trust me; it is a look you don't see often. He started with 15 acres and ended up with 2500 acres. The only money we put into it was from gold he dug from the ground. We ended up with back hoes, bull dozers, water plants and a smelting operation. Once a month Jay would come into Vegas and bring my share of the gold or money or records to show what had happened. I told him not to worry about it...I don't need to see records because I knew he would take a bullet before he would steal or lie. Jay not only DARED TO BE GREAT...he defined greatness. It was July1 when Jay came to my house. He told me the cancer was back and they had only given him a couple of months. He said he didn't want to die in a hospital and ask if he could die in my house. We converted the pool room into a hospital room and Jay moved in. I am telling you this part of the story to illustrate what true integrity is. He promised me that he wouldn't die on my birthday, Aug. 14...and laughed. We spent the next month talking and remembering old times, but by August 1st this 225 lb. giant was down to 90 pounds and he was too weak to even use his talker. On Aug 10th he kept asking me what the date was...we both knew the end was only days away. On Aug 14th, my birthday, his pain medication was no longer working and I begged him to let go...let it end. He motioned for his talker. I handed it to him and he found the strength to say. I gave my word I would not ruin your birthday forever. I don't lie. There was a clock over his bed and at 12:01 Aug. 15, Jay Madison Finlay passed away ....to his dying breath a man of his word. If ever you might think, a white lie won't hurt, or it might be ok to take something that is not yours.... I hope you remember this story and this man whose code said, "The only true value a person can have is their integrity and honor ".

<u>Wally Zass Appreciate every day while you can</u> Wally Westin was a comic. He worked in the last days of Vaudeville. He was working in Jack Ruby's club when John F. Kennedy was assassinated. He had legally changed his last name to Zass because he thought it was funny that people were going out to see Wally Zass. When I met Wally, he was working as an MC at Carmichael's Strip Club in Florida. We instantly became friends because I loved show business and this guy had more stories and history than anyone I had ever met. He liked me because I wanted to hear ALL of his stories. They were all great stories. For example, he had testified before the Warren Commission that he had met Lee Harvey Oswald in Jack Ruby's office. It was a Friday night and Wally was going into the office to be paid. There was a poker game going on and Wally was introduced to the players. He remembered Lee Oswald because he remarked how much he enjoyed Wally's

show. Wally's testimony was cut from the report because it did not fit with the story that Oswald and Ruby did not know each other. After moving from Florida, Wally and I lost contact. Fifteen years later I was again doing a show in the Florida town where we had met. I tried to look Wally up hoping I would not find that he had passed. I found him. He was living in a senior home near Destin Florida and when I called, I was able to speak with one of the nurses. I explained who I was and that Wally and I were old friends. I told her I wanted to invite him to a show if he was able to attend. This nurse told me that she had heard that Wally had once been in show business and would try to pass on the invitation. She told me not to expect him because for the last year, he had barely moved and had not spoken since she worked there. I was extremely sad to learn what had happened to my friend. That night, 15 minutes before the show, a lady in white nurses' uniform came backstage and told me Wally Zass was in the audience. I had him wheeled to a front table and could not wait to introduce my old friend to a new audience. I knew he would appreciate the introduction but did not expect him to be able to respond with anything but a smile. Not only did he smile… he stood up and waved. I said, "Wally, do you have any stories for us?" He almost ran to the stage and began his routine. Within a matter of seconds, he had the audience in the palm of his hand and like the master he was, he knew exactly what to do with them. Wally Zass did almost 20 minutes that night and to be perfectly honest, he was a hard act to follow. His nurse had tears streaming down her face. About two weeks later I got a call from his nurse. Wally has passed away. She told me that for the last few weeks of his life, Wally was actually happy. The applause and laughter he had generated that night with me had been enough to carry him through till his next big gig on the other side.

JACK BERRY I cannot end this session talking about great entertainers without mentioning my friend and mentor Jack Berry. Jack gave me my career. All the things I learned from other people, Jack had tried to tell me but I was to thick to listen. I saw my first hypnosis show in 1968. I was a student at the University of Georgia on spring break in Atlanta Georgia. Jack Berry was performing at a club called Earls Place just outside of Atlanta. I was blown away. To his friends, Jack's nickname was spooky eyes because of his deep piercing stare. Jack Berry, along with his contemporaries Dr. Dean, Pat Collins, Ginger Corte and Reveen, paved the way for me and you to make a living doing what we love. It is not an understatement to say, seeing Jack Berry's show changed my life. To say I was enthralled is an understatement. About two weeks into my skeptical investigation, I went on stage with Jack and became a believer. When I returned to school, I changed my major and began my lifelong quest to learn everything I could about hypnosis. Several years later when I decided to learn stage hypnosis; I sought out the man who had originally captured my attention, Jack Berry who to me always will be " Mr. Hypnosis".

CHAPTER SEVEN

SKITS AND ROUTINES

Before continuing, there is something that I need to get off my chest. Recently, on a public forum I expressed my opinion about certain practices happening in the hypnosis industry. I stated my opinion and stated very clearly why that was my opinion. Someone, who shall remain nameless took exception and thought I was attacking him. Rather than refute what I had said, he began a rant about how anyone who disagreed with his style was a jealous hater. He offered no solid reasons for doing the acts I took exception with, and began name calling and spouting tired clichés about his huge successes. At the time I made the observation, I was reacting to a video someone had sent me to review. After reading the rants, I chose to withdraw from the "discussion" because arguing is not an exchange of ideas but rather egos shouting out to be noticed. Now, I recount this unpleasant encounter here to make a point. The ideas I present here for your approval, have been well thought out and I have what I feel to be solid reasons for employing them. If you do not agree....do not use them. The point is, you should have a reason for everything you do in a hypnosis show. I have always done it this way is not a reason. So, and so does it this way is not a reason. If you can give me a reason why something I am telling you might be wrong, I will listen and if your arguments are sound, I will acknowledge it...and change. My way of doing things certainly is not the only way and I would never espouse such a ridiculous notion. I will however always point out to those who have an inclination to listen when I think something is horribly wrong. That is why I am including here the Face Book post that caused such ranker. Submitted for your consideration:

 "This is something for you to consider when you are defining your style. Would you toss the American Flag on the ground? Probably not, because it is disrespectful. Would you pick up a French fry from a dirty floor and eat it? Probably not, because it is not sanitary. Would you put on your best suit of clothes and roll in the dust? Probably not, because you are not a pig. So why I ask would you treat the people who trust you with their safety and well-being with less respect than these inanimate objects. Well, it gets a laugh. So, does farting, but as a hypnotist you should have enough class not to do either on stage, I understand, sometimes someone falling is unavoidable and you should always do your best to keep that from happening. To me, and this is only my opinion, laying your volunteers out on the floor transforms them from your volunteers to your victims. When you "floor" your volunteers, you are no longer saying these people are the stars, you are saying look at how powerful I am. You are making the show about you and not about them. If that is your attitude, so be it...after all it is your circus."

I said all that to say this, as you are writing and picking the bits you are going to do, please have the well-being of your volunteers foremost in your mind. Let's get started. These routines are offered here only to spark your imagination. Build on them

COLD The wording should go something like this, "Everyone on stage, I just received word from management here at the club. They tell me someone has locked the air conditioner on high and it is starting to get very cold in this room. Already it is down to about 5 degrees. You are so cold, you will cuddle up with anything you can find. You don't care if it is a man, a woman or a chair...you will just get cuddled up with anything you can find. It's getting colder now...even colder... and the sprinkler system just went off and you can feel the water droplets hitting you." At this point my assistant shoots a water gun over the row of volunteers and as they feel the droplets hitting them, they do in fact begin to cuddle even harder. Once again...you said it and it happened.

ORCHESTRA I don't do this particular bit because almost everyone does it. It is, however, a very funny and effective opening routine. Everyone on stage is out and you say: "Everyone on stage, you are a fine classical musician all performing here tonight for this very appreciative audience. The better you play, the louder this audience responds. Your instrument is in your lap. Pick up your instrument now. Tonight, you will play better than you have ever played. Your instrument...whether it be a drum, tuba, trumpet, bass, or cymbals (you are actually giving them ideas here about what instrument they have). Pick up your instrument now as you just begin to play" ...START MUSIC NOW". Continue with encouragement as you seemingly conduct the orchestra.... maybe have the music speed up or slow down. The biggest mistake I see being to cut. You are doing a generic bit anyway, so changing the music you use will not really make it yours so make sure the piece you select is recognizable. Also, move about the stage and draw attention to your more animated players.

COLD IN BED WITH TEDDY BEAR I wrote this bit to get away from the hot and cold opener. It has all the necessary elements but is a little different. Everyone on stage is out and you say: "Everyone one stage, you are home in bed getting all snuggled up under the covers. The window in your room is open and it is really cold outside. You are starting to get very cold. What you feel in the bed next to you is your teddy bear. Your bear is really warm. Just get all cuddled up next to your Teddy Bear. That's the way. Just cuddle up. That makes you feel better. It is raining outside and the cold rain is blowing in. You feel the droplets on you and your bear is getting wet. UH OH...the stuffing is coming out of your bear. Quick, push the stuffing back in your bear."

HOT This can be used as an extension of the cold skit or as a stand-alone opener. "The temperature is changing and it's starting to get really warm. In fact, it is downright hot. It's really hot now, especially the shoes. The shoes are the hottest thing about you. Get the shoes off. They are burning your feet. And the socks...man, those socks are on fire, get those socks off. Shoes and socks off, that's starting to cool you down." The beautiful part of this bit is that you are setting up your next routine. They have their shoes and socks off. Go to your best volunteer, pick up his sock look at him and say as you hand him his sock, "This might surprise you my friend but you are going to find as you try to put this sock on...you cannot do it. It will go to the left of your foot, it will go to the right of your foot, it might hang on your big toe...it just won't go on." Hand him his sock as you repeat the suggestion. As soon as he starts having trouble with the socks, move on to do something else with another volunteer. After about 1 minute, come back to him and ask why he is trying to put his gloves on his feet. "No wonder they won't fit on your feet, those are gloves not socks. Put them where they are supposed to be and they will fit just fine." Are you starting to see how such a generic routine can be built upon to make it a major bit? Now it is not just hot and cold wide awake but a developing comedic riff. All these skits are ended with a simple...." Everyone... 1...2....3...WIDE AWAKE! What the heck are you folks doing?" Your next skit should be an individual. You will use the person who was most responsive in your opening bit. Most shows today use all or mostly group skits and after about 15 minutes, the entire show becomes extremely boring. We will discuss why this is so later.

GAMES WITH NAMES I love this routine because from this one bit you can create running gags that can be used for callbacks throughout the entire show. The basis for all these bits is a simple throwaway routine. A throwaway is a simple bit that gets a quick laugh. In many cases, as with this, the throwaway can be expanded to achieve some hysterical moments. Approach the guy you have determined by your opening bit to be the best. You say. "let's meet everyone. we'll start with you. Sir, what's your name you don't remember", and put the microphone in his face. DO NOT PUT HIM OUT AND SAY, "WHEN I AWAKEN YOU AND ASK YOU YOUR NAME YOU WILL NOT REMEMBER" BECAUSE FRANKLY THAT JUST LOOKS STUPID. This is a throwaway, make it happen fast because now you are going to build on it. As soon as he pauses and looks confused, turn to the audience and ask who he is with. Ask them his name. Let's say it's 'Jack.' Turn back to him and say, "What's your name, Jack, you don't remember". Ideally you don't want him to say anything...just look confused. You do not need to put him out to give a suggestion and to the audience it looks much more impressive if you don't. Now from this quick setup you can go in a dozen different direction and a different direction every show.

NAME ON TIP OF TONGUE Here we are expanding on the name bit. You say, "I think I can help you out. You almost know the name. It is right on the tip of your tongue. Check and see. If you could just get the tongue out far enough to read it. It's right there on the tip of your tongue. See if you can get it out just a little further." To end the bit, touch his forehead and say, "sleep."

WHATEVER NAME YOU HEAR, THAT IS YOUR NAME Another bit building on that throwaway is: "Upon awakening sir, you still don't remember your name, but when you hear anyone else say their name, you will realize THAT' S YOUR NAME! You will be really proud that you have remembered the name and will come to me no matter where I am on stage to tell me." Then, approach a girl and ask her name. When she says it, go back to the guy and ask his name again. He will say the girls name. Do this several times and he will give you a different name every time.

HAPPY BIRTHDAY Another way to play off of the lost name. Put the nameless guy back out. And give the following suggestion. "Sir, upon awakening, you realize that remembering your name is a problem you have had your entire life. You have found a solution. Whenever you need to remember your name, all you have to do is sing out loud HAPPY BIRTHDAY TO YOU HAPPY BIRTHDAY TO YOU, HAPPY BIRTHDAY DEAR

_____ and at that point you will remember the name and can say it." Repeat this suggestion twice. Wake him and ask his name.... he should start singing happy birthday. Always later in the show, before you ask him name again, say to the audience..." I wonder if the birthday thing still works"....otherwise he will have forgotten all about it." This is a good running gag.

CELEBRITY This is another throwaway that can be a great running gag. I find for some reason it works better with a guy. This bit is also useful early in the show because it trains the audience the applaud. "Sir, upon awakening you know exactly who you are. You are none other than.... pick a celebrity, in this case we'll say Justin Bieber....everyone here is your fan. Whenever you hear applause, it is your fans applauding for you.... Justin Bieber...You will stand up, wave to your fans and let them know how much you appreciate them. Justin, if anyone wants an autograph, you'll be more than happy to sign it for them. Whenever you hear applause, it's your fans applauding for you. You'll stand and wave to your fans. Wide Awake!" Ladies and gentlemen, what about a huge round of applause for your stars tonight. Oh, and did I mention Justin Bieber is here? Give it up for Justin!" Let this bit run throughout the entire show. Every time the audience claps, he stands and waves.

TALKING HAT If someone on stage is wearing a hat, this is another great running gag. "Upon awakening, you who I am touching. Any time you see me touch my forehead, you will hear a little voice coming from the inside of your hat. The little voice is saying, "Hey, can you let me out of here?!" When you look in your hat, there is nothing there but every time you see me touch my forehead, you will again hear the little voice saying, "Hey, can you let me out of here?!" No hats? Someone is probably wearing a shirt with a picture of an animal or person. Make the person on their shirt talk to them or the animal have an accident in their lap.

DANCERS Time for a group skit. Put everyone on stage out and set up the dance. Twist, Charleston, YMCA, Chicken dance. "Upon awakening, the next music you hear and any time you hear this music, you have the uncontrollable desire to get up out of your seat and begin dancing this new dance the (YMCA). You will dance better than you have ever danced in your life. Everyone, eyes open, feeling wonderful" Ladies and gentlemen, a big round of applause for your stars......oh, did I mention Justin Bieber? I think I'll let our stars rest a bit and share some of my favorite music. Hit it! " Music starts. It is a good idea to stop and start this a few times and you might also throw in a suggestion while they are dancing. For example, "Wow, you just realized you forgot to get dressed...quick...cover up.... you are totally naked....but you just gotta dance." or "you just lost all your rhythm" or "Uh OH you were moving to hard and your belly button fell off." The point I am trying to make here is, if you are doing generic material, don't just put em out give a suggestion and then wake em up. Build each bit into something unexpected and funny. A magician does a trick and then takes a bow. A hypnotist creates a show from strangers for strangers. When the audience is laughing until they cry, then take a bow.

SHOE THIEF "Sir, upon awakening, the thought foremost in your mind is your love for shoes. You have never been able to get enough shoes. You realize these other people on stage would never miss their shoes if you were to snitch (don't say steal) them while they are sleeping. But you are going to have to hide them someplace on your person, somewhere on your body so you can get out of here with them. Upon awakening, you are the world's most clever shoe snitcher. Wide awake." Then proceed to go to the other people on stage putting them out one at a time. Every time you put someone out, you comment on how cool their shoes are. Point them out to the shoe thief and encourage him to hide them under his shirt or someplace else on his person.

BODYBUILDERS "Upon awakening guys, you are all world champion body builders. We are here tonight at the Mr. Universe competition. You will take the stage and begin flexing and showing off those muscles." DO NOT LET A HEAVY GUY GET HIS SHIRT OFF AND BE EMBARRASSED. Make at least one guy a special foot model and have him show off his highly developed feet.

IN LOVE WITH THE HYPNOTIST (Point of interest, this is a bit I got from Preston. He was 7 feet tall and very, very good. He passed away a few years ago. I traded him my talking teddy bear bit for it) "Everyone on stage, we are going to have a break in the show. During this break I will be playing some beautiful music. While it is playing, I might invite some of you to dance with me. I might invite some of you to dance abs should you be one of the people I invite to dance, you will discover as we are dancing that you are absolutely head over heels in love with the hypnotist. After that, should you then see me dancing with someone else, you will become extremely jealous. You cannot use any form of violence but your ever expression will show how jealous you are. Everyone, wide awake." turn to the audience and say, "While our stars are taking a break, I'd like to share one of my favorite songs. Slow music starts. For the 1st few dances, dance a few moments with someone of the opposite sex. While you are slow dancing, you can give off mic suggestions for them to either run their fingers through your hair or they will be very jealous if you dance with someone else. On the 3rd or 4th dance, you dance with someone of the same sex. You might give the suggestion that they grab your butt. When they do, Yell "Wide Awake!"

SHELDON'S CHAIR This is another variation of the celebrity on stage routine. "Upon awakening, you are Sheldon Cooper from "The Big Bang Theory". You realize every few minutes that someone on this stage is in your chair. This is absolutely not acceptable. You will make them move. And Sheldon, whenever you hear applause, it is the Nobel Committee applauding for you. You will stand, wave and bow." So, here we have looked at 15 routines. Every bit, every routine can be expanded in countless direction. Work on being able to smoothly integrate all of these into your show and get comfortable. You do not need nor should you ever use a skit list. A list tends to make you want to follow the same path every time. A hypnotist should be a master of improv and let instinct point the direction

PROFESSOR MARVEL'S WONDERFUL ELIXER Set up is everything here. Your prop is a small spray bottle filled with water. Put everyone out and talk to the audience. As you are explaining to the audience about this wonderful new product, you are actually giving the suggestion to your subjects. You turn to the audience and say. "Ladies and Gentlemen, recently I sow a wonderful new product advertised on television. You see something on television that you just have got to have. Well, that's what happened to me with Professor Marvels wonder tonic. It does everything. Whatever you need, it will do for you. It will make you pretty, strong, smart, sexy.... whatever you want. You simple decide what you want it to do...and apply. This stuff is wonderful. Here, let me show you. Everyone on stage, upon awakening, I will be spraying some of Professor Marvels Elixir on your hands...when you tell it what you want it to do and apply it...it always works. 1,2, 3...wide awake." Go to each person and ask them what they want the elixir to do for them. You can use off microphone queuing if you like to get some funny responses...example, I want bigger boobs.... well I guess you know where to apply it then. After everyone has

applied it and is getting some response, start to read out the side effects. This will also happen to them. Note: If you are still taking 20 people on stage this bit will run too long to do with everyone so just do it with maybe 5 or 6 people.

CELL PHONES Today everyone owns a cell phone and will usually have it with them on stage so you should take advantage of the prop they bring for you. We have already talked about the shoe phone which is a bit I wrote back in he days of the "Get Smart" television series. Here are a few more ideas using the cell phone.

a. Most phones today have cameras so have them taking selfies and making their best "Duckface".

b. Have a sound effect ringtone and every time they hear it, it is their phone ringing. When they answer it will be one of these things: It is someone informing them they have won the lottery. It is their ex calling to borrow money. it is an obscene call...and they like it. It is a prank call asking about prince Albert in a can. The possibilities here are limited only by your imagination.

c. They are a contestant on a game show. Have them call a friend to get help with an answer for a really simple question that has them stumped. This could be a funny time to use a call back and have the call a friend to ask what their name is (can't remember name skit) is or how many fingers they have (number 6 is missing skit) or they only speak Chinese when they have their friend on the line. This could be a high-tech version of the old prank call, only this time the prankster is also being punked. This is actually such a funny idea that I think I will add this to my show using this explanation to the audience. "Ladies and Gentlemen, when I was a kid one of the great games was to make stupid prank calls. Some of you probably did it too. Remember, 'is your refrigerator running or do you have prince Albert in a can?' Problem is, I never grew up and I still like to do it....but now I do it this way. You who I am touching, in a moment I will awaken you and you will decide you need to make some calls. It is very important that you do it now. You will begin to call the people on your contact list and when they answer....dadada..you get the idea here.

SEXY THOUGHT This is done with a young man usually between 17 and 25 years old. Make sure he is seated between two attractive girls. The wording should be something like this. Upon awakening, any time you have any thought that has anything to do with sex or romance, you will immediately relax, collapse and go back deep asleep as you are now. Wide awake." Look at him and point to the girl next to him. As soon as he looks at her, he will "sleep". If necessary, when he looks at her, off mic, you say sleep. This can be a running gag that you can use throughout the show.

LONG PRETTY HAIR Have you ever had a bald guy on stage? Put him out and explain that upon awakening, the thing that he is most proud of in his long beautiful hair. He will love running his fingers through it at tossing his head to make his hair flip. Give him a brush and have him smooth out the tangles.

CHINESE RAPPERS This bit was created by Michelle Van Ree. I was training Michelle at the Stampede one year and without warning handed her the Microphone and said, "you are on". Michelle relates and talks to the audience and thinks on her feet. The challenge I gave her was to come up with something off the top of her head. you can still hear. I was in the middle of the "only speak Chinese bit when I handed her the Mic. She immediately picked up on the action an made them all rappers...but they still only spoke or sang in Chinese. The result was hilarious and has become one of her staple routines.

FEET STUCK I have seen so many people doing this wrong. Done properly it cannot fail. I mentioned earlier that I use this usually with my worst volunteer to as a convince and to turn him into one of the best "Stars". If you tell someone their feet are stuck and step back 5 out of 10 times they will not be stuck. However, if you tell them exactly where to place each foot, then when you tell him his right foot is stuck, your bodies are touching making it impossible for him to shift his weight in order to lift the foot. This is so subtle, even the person you are doing it with will not notice the balance problem. Next when show him where to place his other foot I have my hand on his shoulder and gently keep him from shifting his weight so that he can move, it is a matter of controlling his balance. From now on, this guy will be great.

KID IN LOVE If you are working fairs, kids can not only be your best stars but almost always their parents buy the video. The problem is material for kids. With kids, it is even more important than usual to keep the bit simple, so that they have to do very little to get a great reaction. I usually save the missing number for kids because for some reason it is just cuter when a kid discovers he has extra fingers. In this bit all the kid has to do is turn his head and smile to get a great audience reaction. The suggestion is simply, upon awakening, the girl next to you is the most beautiful girl and you cannot take your eyes off her. She is sooo beautiful.

FLASHER FOR ADULT ONLY SHOWS I will be including one routine each month for the adult show. This one could actually be used at PG13. The idea came when I saw a fan in the front row who had attended every show I ever did in Calgary. Her name was BA and she was 89 years old, in a wheel chair and she loved to laugh. Simply suggest that someone in the front row is lifting their blouse and flashing them.

TALKING TALLYWACKER ...Very Adult. The skit is self-explanatory. The one thing I want to mention is when doing adult material, there is no need to be vulgar. For example, you will notice I use the word tallywacker. That is a cute word. I could have said cock or dick and the meaning would have been the same but the feeling would be different. In an adult show, it is perfectly permissible to use adult language when the situation calls for it or if it makes the be funnier, but don't swear just to use dirty words so you can call it an adult show. Upon awakening you will begin to hear a voice coming from the area of your lap. It is your tallywacker talking to you. It has never done that before. After a few seconds you will realize that if you can hear it...so can everyone else. Anthony Cools took this idea and changed it to TALKING COCHEE, which I think is funnier. Note he could have used a more vulgar term but he chose the funnier word coochie.

WHAT'S MY NAME? This is simply an expansion on the 'can't remember name' bit. But now you tell him that he is on a game show and may call any person he wants who is not in the audience to help him remember his name. This is a very funny bit but many times it gets bogged down waiting for someone on the other end to answer the phone. I always tell them not to use the speaker phone because it makes my speakers buzz. It does not of course but I do not want the audience to hear in case I have to use the off-mic queuing. I am holding the mic near the volunteer making the call so any thing I say will not be heard by the audience. If after several rings no one answers I simply say in a quiet voice, "They just answered so go ahead and talk and ask your question." Keep in mind, all I need to get the comedic effect for the audience is for the person to ask a friend what his name is and it does not matter if that friend is really on the phone or not.

CINDY Everyone nowadays has a cell phone. The bit is just this. I have one guy pull out his cell phone and call everyone in the memory of his phone to tell them that he now wants them to call him Cindy because it makes him feel pretty. The setup is obvious in the clip but what is not obvious is the off mic queuing I am doing when the microphone is in his face. Watch when I ask his name and move the mic towards him after a few seconds of not getting the response I want, I scratch my nose.... what I am really doing is telling him that his friend just answered....talk to him.

HEADACHE This can be either used as a 'throw away filler bit' or as a running gag throughout the show. In the set up I tell the person that their head feels great, better than it has ever felt and they knows it is because the shoulder (or lap if it is an adult show) that they just had their head on is magical and any time they place their head on that shoulder they experiences euphoria...and whenever they hear a certain song (put your head on my shoulder) they again want to have that wonderful feeling. The result is someone rubbing their head on the shoulder of the person next to them like a cat. This is especially effective if the person whose shoulder is being used has been given the suggestion that the person next to them smells bad or is getting fresh.

JERRY SPRINGER This is from an adult show and the language is strong. There is nothing wrong with doing an adult show as long as EVERY MEMBER OF THE AUDIENCE KNOWS WHAT TO EXPECT. You can do adult material without being offensive or crude Do not try to throw in adult material at a regular show just for good measure. You probably won't offend anyone but why take the chance. I am including this because in this bit off mic queuing is used extensively. If they say the dirty stuff it's ok. I might have prompted them to say it but I look always as shocked as the audience. Although this is a group skit, you should take note that I still spotlight individuals. Group skits to not all have to be pure chaos.

This morning when I sat down at the keyboard, I looked at the items on my desk and decided to write some new bits either using or inspired by these items. This is the result. The items on my desk were:

1.a pair of sunglasses 2. a bottle of water 3. a mouse 4. A part from a door 5. An i pad

SUNGLASSES Well the obvious thing to do with a pair of glasses is to make them x-ray specs. and I want to avoid being that mundane and obvious. We wear sun glasses when we are out in the sun...driving to avoid glare...or just want to be cool. Let's go with the last one. "You sir who I am touching, upon awakening, I am going to give you a very special gift. This gift was actually given to me many years ago by a dear friend. His name is Authur Fonzarelli...you may know him as "THE FONZ". It was this very pair of sun glasses that made The Fonz so cool. In fact, these are magical sunglasses that makes anyone who wears them SUPER COOL ....and they will do just that for you whenever you put them on. You will be irresistible to women and admired by men. You don't want to wear them all the time because you can overdose on cool. You will wear them whenever you feel the need to be cool." From this point on you basically have a Jekyll and Hyde. This can be a running gag throughout the show

BOTTLE OF WATER The obvious thing to do with a bottle of water is to make it booze. Let's not go there. "Sir upon awakening you are extremely thirsty. You will ask me if I can get you something to drink. Of course, because I want all of my stars to be comfortable, I will get you a bottle of water. This will make you happy and you will be anxious to have a drink. Apparently, somehow your swallowing mechanism has been turned off. You want to drink but the water just will not go down your throat. It goes in your mouth fine but for some reason you just can't swallow." Wake him up, give him the bottle of water when he asks and then move on. As soon as he has a mouthful of water, go over and ask if that was refreshing. Obviously when he tries to talk, the water spills out. after a few tries, I would suggest that the reason he cannot swallow is because his ears are too tight and if he were to loosen the ears a few notches back, he would be able to swallow fine.

A COMPUTER MOUSE Hmmmm. When I got my first computer and was unpacking the box, the instructions told _____ me that I had a mouse. I had no idea what a mouse was or why my new computer needed one. "You who I am touching, upon awakening you will find in your lap a very mysterious object. You have NO idea what this object is but you instinctively it is a very sophisticated and important device. This device might actually be one of the most important inventions ever. You need to figure out what it is." This would be a great time to use "off mic" queuing. Maybe tell them it is a phone for contacting aliens.... maybe it is a sex toy (if adult show)...maybe it is a piece of jewelry.

A PIECE FROM A DOOR It is the piece from a door latch that slides into the hole in the door frame. Basically, it is a piece of metal with a button, so we will go with the button idea. A "that was easy" button from the office supply would work just as well. "Upon awakening, I am going to give you a special gift. It is a magic button. Whenever the button is pushed, whoever is holding the device can see through clothing for five seconds. This will really make you smile...big. It is really neat to have such a device. The only drawback is there is a price to pay for using it. whenever the button is pushed it will also cause a mild electrical shock in the butt of the user. It will probably be worth it. The shock is quick and only makes you jump out of your seat a little. You can't wait to try it." This idea actually has some possibilities for use throughout the show.

An I-PAD I would put really goofy pictures of cartoon characters on the pad so they can scroll through them. As they scroll through them, they will recognize different family members and share with the audience treasured stories or memories about this family member in this photo. If it is an adult show they will recognize former lovers and will discuss their sexual prowess.

Five items were on my desk this morning. It took less than 1/2 hour to write 5 bits using these props or items as stimuli to get creative. Probably, if done right 3 or 4 of these could become main routines. Explain to me (not really...you should explain to yourself) why you are still doing the same stuff as everyone else...in every show.

PART 2

UNDERSTANDING HYPNOSIS AND SELF HYPNOSIS

An easy to understand book about Hypnotism

BY

Legendary Hypnotist

TERRY STOKES Sr.

Chapter ONE

Chapter TWO

Chapter THREE

PREFACE -

By
Terry Stokes

As your career as a stage hypnotist progresses you will be called upon more and more to discuss the actual science of hypnotism. In interviews and even private conversation you are expected to be an expert. I have found that sadly, very few hypnotist have any real idea about what hypnosis is and therefore can not discuss it intelligently. Many have taken a weekend course and start doing shows (badly I might add) but have no real knowledge about the tool they are working with.

Granted, you do not need to understand electricity to turn on a light switch but if the power goes out, it would be nice to know why. You are going to be called on to help people with problems and will probably want to put out a line of self-help programs, this section will get you started in the right direction.

My interest in hypnosis began many years ago when I saw stage hypnotist Jack Berry perform his nightclub show in Atlanta, Georgia. That night, hypnosis became my life's passion. The passion has not waned over the years and my respect for the science of hypnosis continues to grow.

I began my professional career in hypnosis as a therapist at the Atlanta Hypnosis Institute. One night, as I told a weight control class that they should be doing what they really want to do most, I stopped and thought, "If this is such good advice, why don't I take it myself?" My dream was to become an entertainer. So, I sold my interest in the business to my partners, wrote a show, and have been touring with it ever since. It really was good advice. I am aware that many practicing hypnotists frown upon or even condemn stage hypnosis, but I want to say that I have learned more about the science of hypnosis as a stage hypnotist than I ever learned in college or workshops or from textbooks.

Without the stage hypnotist, the art and science of hypnosis would have withered and died while awaiting official sanction. It is also my belief that I help more people in one

performance as a stage hypnotist than I could in weeks working as a therapist. If for one hour I can make 500 people forget all of their worries and problems and laugh…. I have performed a very therapeutic service.

Over the years, I have taught hundreds of classes and have worked with thousands of students in workshops throughout the United States and Canada.

I always begin with two questions:

(1) Have you ever read or studied about hypnosis?

(2) Have you ever been hypnotized?

Invariably, the answers are the same: "Yes, I have read about hypnosis," and "No, I don't think I've ever been hypnotized."

These two answers do not go together. Those who have read or studied about hypnosis should know that everyone has been hypnotized. So, either they do not understand what they are reading, or the books they are reading are incorrect or confusing.

I believe the real answer is somewhere in the middle. A few people say they have studied a subject when actually they have read no more than an article or two. Most, however, have actually read a great deal about hypnosis, but it was unfortunately outdated or technically confusing material.

Many of the most modern texts are merely copies of outdated works, and poor or wrong ideas are passed from text to text, Understanding Hypnosis and Self-Hypnosis often unchallenged. The books that do challenge old concepts are usually too technical for the nonprofessional.

One notable exception to this is Self Hypnosis and Other Mind Expanding Techniques by Charles Tebbetts. This is an excellent work and a must have for any complete hypnosis library. I have used Tebbetts' book extensively in the preparation of this manuscript.

Because hypnosis is possibly the most promising tool available for developing human potential, I feel there is a great need for a simple, easy to understand work on hypnosis. It is my hope to have produced that work in the following pages.

First-time students of hypnosis will discover many, if not all of their preconceived ideas about hypnosis are completely false. Even many practicing hypnotists may find challenges to some of their most basic beliefs about their craft.

For example, until a few years ago, all hypnotists were taught that to achieve a good enough trance level for behavior modification, the hypnotic induction should be at least fifteen minutes long. When seeing a stage hypnotist accomplishing this fifteen-minute task in one minute or less, it was simply shrugged off as fake or a setup.

In this book I will try to share my observations from working with thousands of people every year. I will attempt to answer some of the most basic questions about hypnosis as well as direct the reader in techniques for obtaining maximum benefit from the use of self-hypnosis.

For quick reference, Chapter Six, "Questions and Answers," is a recap of the first five chapters. It is set up so the reader can quickly scan for information.

Best wishes,

~ Terry Stokes

CHAPTER ONE

A BRIEF HISTORY OF HYPNOSIS

Although it was not called hypnosis back then, priests, witchdoctors and healers have used the principles of scientific suggestion throughout history. The oldest reference to hypnosis is found in the "Ebers Papyrus" of ancient Egypt. The Greeks had 'sleep temples' where people came to be healed and were put into a trance-like state.

The science of hypnotism dates back centuries but was not expanded nor its principles used until Friedrich Anton Mesmer generally known as the Father of Hypnosis, developed his theory of animal magnetism. Mesmer believed that a disturbance of equilibrium in a "universal fluid" caused the diseases in human beings, and that all cures could be brought about by re-adjustment of these "invisible fluids."

Although Mesmer produced the hypnotic state many times, he was quite unaware of what he was doing. His theories were wrong, but his relaxation techniques and suggestions of wellbeing did in fact produce what seemed to be remarkable results. It was Mesmer's pupil, Marquis Armond de Puysequr, who actually discovered the hypnotic trance, which he called "artificial somnambulism."

The followers of these two men steadfastly adhered to the erroneous principles of animal magnetism. In 184, Dr. James Braid, a Scottish surgeon, coined the word "hypnosis" which is from the Greek "Hypnos" meaning sleep. Later, Dr. Braid realized his mistake when he found his patients were not really asleep. He actually tried to change the word to "monadism," meaning that the mind had narrowed to one idea. Although this word more accurately described the condition, the term, "hypnosis" had already obtained a good start and unfortunately the idea still persists today that a hypnotized person is asleep.

Over the years, many theories about hypnosis have come and gone and there has never really been a completely acceptable one, nor has there been a truly scientific explanation of what happens in this state. Today, the use of medical hypnosis is widespread around the world. Treatments include: control of pain (i.e., painless childbirth, painless dentistry, and induced anesthesia), moral problems, physical therapy, memory loss, weight loss, stopping smoking, and behavior modification. The list could go on and on.

In law enforcement hypnosis has frequently and successfully been used to cause victims to recall in detail the events of an accident or attack on their person, including events they had forced from their memories or had never correctly observed.

As a final introductory thought, I would like to state that after years of work in the field of hypnosis, I find that the only thing I know for certain is that it works - when other forms of mind experience fall short.

COMMON MISCONCEPTIONS

The science of hypnosis is plagued with misconceptions and misunderstandings. The first step to understanding hypnosis is to get rid of the misconceptions you may have accumulated about it.

Most people fall into one of two categories in what they know about hypnosis:
1) Those who know nothing at all.
2) Those who know a little, but most of what they know is wrong.

Those handicapped by misinformation also fall into two categories:
1) Those that fear hypnosis, believing it is dangerous, supernatural, etc.
2) Those who believe that it is a cure-all for everything, based on a rather magical belief.

As a performing hypnotist, I meet hundreds of people who are actually terrified of me. Waitresses won't look me in the eye, because they think I might hypnotize them without their knowledge. Bank tellers have someone watch them count my money so I cannot use my strange power on them. Although amusing, the futility of explanation is frustrating.

The most common fear and misconception about hypnosis is that of losing control and revealing one's secrets.

A hypnotized person does not lose control. They are not under the control of the hypnotist. ALL HYPNOSIS IS SELF-HYPNOSIS. The hypnotist only leads the subject through the relaxation process and acts as a coach.

If I could hypnotically convince a bank teller to give me extra money, it would be because the teller convinced himself that I could do it. People seem to think they have some horrible monster hidden deep inside that is going to jump out if they are hypnotized. Can't happen, folks! A professional hypnotist is not interested in your secrets, and you would not reveal them anyway. Another common fear many people express is that they will not wake up. When you understand that a hypnotized person is not really asleep, then it follows that not waking up is not a problem. A hypnotized person is aware of every word said and will, in most cases, be aware of everything that happens while hypnotized.

A HYPNOTIZED PERSON IS NOT ASLEEP.

As I travel throughout the United States and Canada, I have the opportunity to meet with many practicing hypnotists. Many tell me that although they have no trouble hypnotizing their clients, they have never themselves been hypnotized. These people should know that not only have THEY been hypnotized, but so has every normal person. HYPNOSIS IS A NATURAL FUNCTION OF MIND.

There is nothing magical about hypnotism, though there have been cases where the effects of hypnosis have seemed miraculous, because of the amazing results people have experienced. Everyone has within them the ability to heal cuts, bruises and broken bones. This is not magic; it is normal, and hypnosis is a technique that enables the mind to best use those abilities. It is merely a means of helping you use the natural healing talents of the body.

Many preconceived ideas about hypnosis are so far removed from the truth as to be ridiculous. There is not one Understanding Hypnosis and Self-Hypnosis documented case of harm coming to anyone as the result of the use of controlled hypnosis.

When people tell me they are afraid of hypnosis, I am reminded of the story of the old man who objected to the purchase of a new chandelier for the church. When asked to explain the reasons for his objections, he replied, "Well, in the first place, nobody in this here church can spell it. In the second place, nobody here knows how to play the darned thing. And finally, what this church really needs is more lights." Fear is the result of ignorance and faulty information. Understanding the true nature of hypnosis should eliminate any and all fears.

Hypnotism is neither metaphysics nor religion, although it may explain some of the miraculous cures affected by sincere faith healers. It is not contrary to the teachings of any of the major religions, and is in fact, used by most of them. Any thought or idea repeated at length in solemn surroundings deepens faith by subconscious affirmation, and this is hypnosis.

Most people are hypnotized every day of their life. While reading a book, watching TV, or any time the critical thought process is suspended.

HYPNOSIS DEFINED

The most popularly accepted definition of hypnosis is, "Hypnosis is an altered state of consciousness characterized by heightened suggestibility and ultra relaxation." Not only is this definition vague, it is misleading.

For example, consider a mob scene where a person is worked into frenzy. The mob members lose all sense of critical thought and go out and hang the target of the frenzy. The mob members were highly suggestible and followed the suggestions of the mob leader.

But were they ultra relaxed? No. Well then, were they hypnotized? Yes, because the critical thought process was suspended and they were responding to the outside suggestion. A STATE OF HYPNOSIS EXISTS WHENEVER THE CRITICAL THOUGHT PROCESS HAS BEEN SUSPENDED.

This example seems to contradict my earlier statement that a hypnotized person is not out of control and hypnosis is completely safe. That the contradiction exists makes necessary to introduce two new terms. The above example is what we will term accidental hypnosis. It is the automatic suspension of critical thought, allowing random suggestions to be accepted and acted upon. It is what happens to most people when they do not control their own subconscious mind. If you do not control your subconscious, it will control you. Stated another way; if you do not control the ideas programming your subconscious, any success you achieve will be purely accidental.

The other term is controlled hypnosis. This is what most people think of as hypnosis. It involves an intentional suspension of the critical factor, so a suggestion can be accepted for some specific purpose.

So in effect, not only does a person experiencing controlled hypnosis not lose control, they actually gain control over a part of their behavior motivation.

HOW IT FEELS TO BE HYPNOTIZED

When you experience controlled hypnosis, whether by a professional hypnotist or doing it yourself, the result is the same. Every muscle in the body becomes pleasantly relaxed and all tension disappears. You feel this relaxation in various degrees from one hypnotic experience to another.

With practice, you will be able to relax completely in a matter of seconds. After your nerves and muscles relax, your mind also lets go, and although you remain aware of noises and activity around you, they do not disturb your tranquil mood in any way.

You can think and bring critical thought back if you desire, but only an emergency triggers such a desire because you prefer to continue enjoying your relaxed mood. You do not pass out or become unconscious; you remain conscious of where you are and what you are doing, but you generally feel too relaxed and comfortable to want to think about it.

You can come back to complete conscious awareness at any time you choose. For instance, if the phone rings, you can discard your trance and answer the phone, without remaining in hypnosis.

No one has ever been unable to come out of hypnosis, and the sensational stories that you might hear about people stuck in hypnosis are completely unfounded. A few neurotics have been known to enjoy the pleasant, relaxed state so much that they refuse to awaken at another's command, but they could do so any time they wished. This again illustrates the point that all hypnosis is self-hypnosis; if they refuse to return to a normal state of consciousness, they eventually go into natural sleep and awaken as usual when rested.

As a performing hypnotist, this situation can cause unwarranted concern and panic from uniformed on-lookers. As a performer, my job is not to educate but to entertain. Were I to leave a subject alone and allow them to sleep it off, I would appear to be negligent. Therefore, in a show situation, I simply whisper in to the subject's ear something like, "I know you are enjoying the very restful feeling you are experiencing, but many people are becoming concerned. In a moment, I will count from one to three, at which time you will awaken and wave to thunderous applause. You will continue to feel wonderful." The person is aware of what is going on, and I simply give them a reason to want to awaken.

During a ten- or fifteen-minute trance, both your body and mind become revitalized, and you awaken feeling physically refreshed and emotionally serene. You will have renewed energy without tension.

Here are some sensations that you may experience while in hypnosis: Your arms or legs may seem to float a few inches above the floor. They may feel heavy, as though they were sinking into the floor. You may feel a tingling sensation in the hands or feet. Parts of your body may seem not to exist at all. You might see strange visions or beautifully colored patterns of light. None of these sensations is harmful and all are usually very pleasant.

WHO CAN BE HYPNOTIZED?

Now that you realize hypnosis is not an unnatural state but rather a state the average person slips into and out of every day without realizing it, you should suspect that anyone could be hypnotized.

You suspend critical thought when you become involved watching television, otherwise you would not be able to enjoy the program. Imagine watching a show and reminding yourself, every few minutes that the people on the screen are only actors. BORING! To enjoy the show, you must suspend critical thought and become a part of the action. Is that really hypnosis? Sure it is. That is why TV commercials are effective; we suspend critical thought and become highly suggestible.

Daydreaming is another good example of natural hypnosis. When you are daydreaming, time seems to pass quickly because conscious thought is not active to make judgments about the passing minutes. You may have experienced this phenomenon while driving down the freeway and you suddenly realize that your exit was five miles back.

The point is simply this: 100% OF ALL NORMAL PEOPLE CAN
AND DO EXPERIENCE HYPNOSIS.

THE CONSCIOUS
AND SUBCONSCIOUS MIND

Think of the mind as divided into two parts. Although these two parts of mind work together, they have separate and distinct functions.

The part of our mind that we are most aware of is the conscious mind. The conscious mind is the analytical part of the mind; it makes judgments and decisions. It was this part of your mind that made the decision to purchase this book.

Scientists refer to this part of mind as beta level of thought. The conscious mind has a single function: It makes critical judgments and decisions based on information gathered and stored in the subconscious. The conscious mind analyzes all information we receive through our senses, then passes that information along to the subconscious where it is filed into our mental computer. THE CONSCIOUS MIND MAKES DECISIONS AND CRITICAL JUDGMENTS.

The subconscious mind is, by far, the more powerful of the two levels of mind, although we are usually unaware of its operation. The subconscious is called alpha level of thought. It is our source of energy and motivation, yet is has no ability to analyze and make judgments.

For example, obese individuals might consciously decide they would be happier and healthier if they could control their food intake and reduce their weight, yet they find it impossible to do so. Trying to modify a habit pattern with conscious effort alone is like trying to sweep back the ocean waves; you can do it for a little while, but you will almost surely lose the battle.

Although the conscious mind has the ability to reason and decide on a course of action, unless the sub-conscious agrees Understanding Hypnosis and Self-Hypnosis and directs its energy towards the implementation of those decisions, no amount of willpower exerted by the conscious mind can override the subconscious.

In the past, when you used your conscious or beta level of mind to accomplish something like losing weight or stopping smoking, you probably found it difficult to stay with the program - if you did not reprogram the subconscious portion of your mind as well. On the other hand, when you involve the subconscious or alpha level of thought, the changes just seem to happen automatically.

As already stated, the conscious mind has one basic function: to evaluate and compare each new idea and bit of information it receives before passing it along to the subconscious memory bank. The subconscious mind has at least six basic functions:

1) It stores all memories. Everything that we have ever heard, seen, tasted, smelled or felt is permanently stored in a maze of memory patterns which, when activated, will feed back that information to the conscious mind. Have you ever tried to remember something and the information just would not come? Finally, you give up and say to heck with it - then a few minutes later, the memory pops into your head.

Memories are never stored on a conscious level. You use conscious mind to decide to recall the memory - the conscious mind requests the memory from the subconscious - then waits for its delivery.

2) The subconscious controls all involuntary body functions, such as digestion and the immune and respiratory systems. 3) All habit patterns are controlled by the subconscious. The subconscious also carries out habitual conduct such as driving
a car or tying a tie.

4) The subconscious is the seat of our emotions. Since emotions govern the strength of our desires and our desires govern our behavior, we are the products of our subconscious beliefs. Therefore, we are what we have been programmed to be, and only by learning to change the programming can we change ourselves.

5) The subconscious is the home of imagination. As children, we all have lively imaginations, but as adults, many people begin to suppress their imagination. If you think about it, you are most creative when you are relaxing. That is because critical thought is turned down and the subconscious is allowed to run free of conscious intervention.

When the conscious mind is not active and telling you that logically something is impossible, the subconscious is usually busy finding a solution.

6) The subconscious mind directs our energy. Behavior is merely energy expressed. This energy cannot be destroyed nor can it be created, but it can be directed. Since the subconscious constantly and automatically uses this energy to proceed towards a goal, if you do

not set a goal for it to achieve, it will either choose its own or proceed towards a goal someone else has suggested. Without your direction, it might strive towards illness, failure or some other destructive goal. It always achieves what it sets out to accomplish.

A SIMPLE EXPERIMENT
WITH INSTANT HYPNOSIS

So far, we have talked about what hypnosis is and how it works, but I have learned from teaching classes that no amount of explanation is as effective as a demonstration.

Here is a simple example of instant hypnosis:

A state of hypnosis exists whenever the critical factor of thought has been suspended. This can easily be demonstrated on a person with a headache.

Tell the person to close their eyes as you place your right palm on the person's forehead, with your thumb and middle finger just above the temple area.

Place your left hand behind the person's head with the thumb and fingers touching the top of the neck, just behind the ears.

As you gently begin to massage, say the following:

"I would like you to imagine a war going on inside your head. You can see it, feel it – cannons firing, bombs exploding, soldiers marching. Marching on… and on and on.

Now, focus your attention on their feet. See their feet. Marching..now running. All around them cannons firing and bombs exploding. See the war going on in your head?

In a moment, I am going to count from one to three, and when I reach three, the war will be over.

My hands will become giant magnets and as I pull them away from your head, all the pain and tension will be drawn out into the palms of my hands.

But right now, the war is raging. Bombs exploding. (Slightly increase the pressure and speed of the massage).

ONE, the war is almost over.

TWO, the bombs have stopped.

And THREE, the war is over!"

Now, quickly draw your hands away and say, "How does it feel?"

To their surprise, and perhaps yours too, their headache will be gone. Why? By asking them to use their imagination and visualize the war and soldiers, we forced them to suspend critical thought. We gave them a TV program to watch in their head.

When critical thought was suspended, we slipped them a suggestion: that our hands would be magnets and the pain would be drawn out.

Critical thought would have told them that hands cannot be magnets, but they had suspended critical thought while visualizing the war, so the suggestion was accepted.

PRESTO! Instant hypnosis.

CHAPTER TWO

COMMERCIAL HYPNOSIS
TAPES & CDs

People frequently ask me about commercial hypnosis tapes and CDs. Do they really work? Are they as effective as actually being with the hypnotist? Are they safe?

The answer to all three questions is yes.

As you have already learned, all hypnosis is self-hypnosis, and all the hypnotist does is lead the subject through the process. This relaxation process can be accomplished as well on tape or CD as in person. Actually, in a great many cases, the recording will work better than being with the hypnotist. There are several reasons for this. You can use the recording in the quiet and comfort of familiar surroundings; you can use the recording at your convenience, not when you can get an appointment; and you can use the recording as often as necessary.

The only caution I offer is: be sure the tapes or CDs you purchase are by a qualified professional. There are several good recordings available, but many are produced by nonprofessionals who are often ignorant of the basic rules of effective suggestion. I, of course, recommend my own tapes and CDs and thumb drives.

SELF-HYPNOSIS

Now that you understand the power of the sub-conscious mind and the role that hypnosis can play in reaching and influencing it, the next step is to hypnotize you.

The tools you will use are suggestion, concentration and imagination.

The ability to relax and just let it happen is important. If you try too hard, you will become tense, and that is the opposite of what you are trying to accomplish. If you take a "prove it to me" attitude, you will also impede your progress. Cooperate and you will get your proof.

One reason people have difficulty learning self-hypnosis is that they do not know when they are hypnotized. The very act of questioning requires the use of critical thought and thus breaks the trance state.

The student of self-hypnosis must learn to question after, not during, the hypnotic session. Many times, because they expect something different, people believe they have failed to achieve the trance state, when they have not failed at all.

The light trance, the feeling I just described, is easily obtained with self-hypnosis and is sufficient for reaching the subconscious to plant suggestions. The medium trace naturally follows with practice. The deepest level appears to be, but is not, deep slumber.

Make sure that you avoid an analytical attitude. Analyzing will keep the conscious mind alert, which is self-defeating. If you follow the directions in this chapter and just let it happen, it will.

The best way to learn self-hypnosis is with a post-hypnotic suggestion given by a hypnotist or with the use of a self hypnosis tape or CD. With either method, while in hypnosis you are given suggestions that whenever you repeat a certain procedure, you will re-enter trance. After a few sessions for reinforcement and a few days practice, you will be able to hypnotize yourself with ease.

After learning to successfully hypnotize yourself, you will then be ready to begin giving yourself suggestions. In the next chapter, you will find instructions on the proper procedures for formulating and giving suggestions. They include several suggestions you should incorporate every time you enter hypnosis.

These suggestions are:
0 I will awaken immediately in case of any emergency, alert and completely normal in every way.
0 I will go into hypnosis more quickly and easily every time I practice it.
0 I will awaken in exactly (set your own time limit) minutes.

After you learn the essentials of hypnosis and self-hypnosis, you can easily record your own tapes or CDs, and adapt them to your individual needs.

If you choose to do this, always make the recordings in the second person, as though you were some other person talking to you. Instead of "I am becoming relaxed," say, "You are relaxing." This is the easiest method of hypnotizing yourself.

An "induction" is the dialogue or 'sleep talk' that leads the subject into hypnosis. One of the best inductions for beginners is called Progressive Relaxation. It takes a little longer than some other methods, but it is a superb conditioning technique for the faster methods that can be learned more easily later. It relaxes the body completely; tension is released and the conscious mind drifts in and out of awareness.

Here is how you do it:

First, make a recording of the following script. Make your recording in the second person throughout. It is presented here in the second person, so you may read directly from the book into the microphone.

Begin reading in a soft, relaxed voice. Draw out your voice and pause often between sentences. Your voice and the pace of your speech should suggest drowsiness and relaxation.

After you have recorded the induction and before you record the "wake up" section, you may want to record the suggestions you wish to make. If you prefer, you may leave a blank space on the tape so that you may give yourself mental suggestions.

Next, with the recording made, sit or lie comfortably with your arms parallel to your body. Separate your feet eight to ten inches, so the thighs are not touching. Loosen all tight clothing.

When you play your recording, this is what you should hear:

PROGRESSIVE RELAXATION INDUCTION

"Take a moment and adjust yourself to a comfortable sitting or reclining position.

Loosen all tight clothing and prepare to enjoy a few moments of complete and total relaxation.

Get very comfortable.

Now take a deep breath, and as you let this breath out, close your eyes and allow them to remain closed.

Another deep breath now, and this time, as you let the breath out, begin to relax your entire body.

As we go through this process known as progressive relaxation, you will find that it will become very easy for you to just relax and let go and allow yourself to drift into the most relaxed and peaceful state of mind you have ever experienced.

If you find that your mind starts to wander, or if you fall asleep, don't be concerned, because you're never sleeping subconscious mind will absorb every thought and idea.

You should keep foremost in your mind what we are trying to accomplish, which is simply to achieve a state of total relaxation of mind and body, so that the subconscious mind will be open to the positive suggestions to follow.

Another deep breath, and as you let the breath out, let your thoughts move to your right leg.

Begin now to relax all of the muscles in your right leg. Relax them; allow the muscles to just let go. Imagine a wave of relaxation flowing through your right leg from the sole of your foot... up through your ankle... through

your calf, relaxing every muscle, every nerve and every fiber, and up through your thigh now relaxing.
Your hips, relaxing every muscle as it flows.

Feel this warm relaxing wave flowing down into your left leg now.
Flowing down into the calf now.. relaxing. Flowing on to the very tips of your toes - every muscle every nerve ever fiber so very relaxed.
This wave of relaxation flowing through both of your legs now, leaving them so very heavy and relaxed.
The legs so heavy now you don't even want to move them.
Up through your waist, relaxing every muscle, nerve and every fiber.
Feel this wave flowing around now to the small of your back, relaxing every muscle, just letting go.
Your shoulders relax it seems as if some tremendous weight has been lifted from your shoulders.
And this wave of relaxation flows down into your right arm relaxing every muscle nerve and fiber.
Down into your forearm and wrist now.
Relaxing even down to the very tips of your fingers.
Now begin to relax the muscles in your left arm from the shoulder down through the forearm and wrist relaxing down to the very tips of your fingers.
Every muscle just letting go.
Both arms so very heavy - you don't even want to move them- both arms like a wet rag now.
And around to your chest.
Become aware of your breathing now.

Breathing easily now, and with every word I speak and every breath you take, you will find it will become easier for you to just relax and let go.

Breathing deeply now... and with each breath relaxing even more.

Feel the warm wave flowing around your shoulders now, releasing all tension.

Feel your body becoming so very heavy now.

This wave of relaxation is flowing up through your neck... relaxing... up into your scalp now... relaxing every muscle and tiny nerve.

The muscles around your eyes are relaxing now.

Your eyelids becoming so very heavy.

Today is past.

Tomorrow is a thousand miles away, but right here, right now, there are no worries or cares, only a few moments of complete, total relaxation.

Your eyelids are so very heavy now, it would be too much of an effort to even try to open them, but why try, it feels so very good just to relax....Completely.

The muscles around your jaw and throat are relaxing now.

It feels so good just to relax and let go.

Enjoy this feeling of total relaxation.

All problems are left behind now.'

In a moment, I am going to begin counting from one to ten.

As I do and as you focus on different areas of your body, you will be able to relax more than you have ever imagined.

Just letting go now.
ONE –
Think of your right leg, become aware of all feeling and sensations in your right leg.
Now allow the leg to go heavy. It might start to tingle.
It will become so very heavy that you won't even want to move it.
So heavy and so very, very relaxed.

TWO –
Think of your left leg. Relax it now.
SO… heavy and so very… relaxed.
You don't even want to move it.
Every muscle… every nerve… every fiber… relaxing.
Feel the leg just going limp.
Think of your right arm.
Become aware of every muscle in this right arm.
Relax it now from the shoulder, all the way down to the very tips of your fingers.
Every muscle, heavy and relaxed.
Today is past, tomorrow is a thousand miles away, but right here, right now, there are no problems worries or cares, only a few moments of total relaxation and when you awaken you will feel better than anything you have ever known… feeling now relaxation of mind and body.
Think now of your left arm and begin to relax it.
From the shoulder, all the way down to the very tip of the fingers.
Relaxing.
The arm becoming so very heavy now, it feels so good to relax and let go as you continue to drift deeper into

this most relaxing and peaceful state of mind known as hypnosis.

THREE –

Now bring your mind into perfect harmony with your body.

Allowing all worries and cares to just flow out of your mind; with every word I speak, with every breath you take.

Today is past; tomorrow is a thousand miles away.

Feel the tension flowing out with each breath you exhale.

FOUR –

Now in your mind's eye, try to visualize a clear blue sky.

Now in this sky, see a cloud. This cloud is very soft, very warm.

See it.

Make it a vivid mind experience if you have trouble visualizing this just imagine it there.

FIVE –

Now imagine yourself lying down in this cloud.

Make this a vivid mind experience.

The cloud seems to envelope your entire body.

Feel yourself sinking down into this cloud now.

SO soft.. so very.. Comfortable now.

Just relaxing on this cloud now and the cloud is starting to drift… and as it drifts, you drift with it.

SIX –

It is a warm lazy afternoon and you have nothing to do and nowhere to go so just enjoy drifting now.

So sleepy… now as you just drift off with this could.

Deeper now allowing yourself to just sleep.
SEVEN –
So very… very relaxed.
And EIGHT –

Totally and fully relaxed now. The problems of the day are no more… Your mind is clean and crisp.
NINE –
Still drifting on this soft … and wonderful cloud.
TEN-- just drifting."

At this point, you will begin to give suggestions to your subconscious, either with a pre-recorded message or with mental visualization.
You will use this basic induction in making all of your hypnosis recordings.
In the next chapter, we will discuss how to properly formulate specific suggestions, so for now you should just give the basic suggestions for health and well-being.
Remember, at this point you are only learning to enter trance. With practice, you will not even need the recording and will be able to enter and exit trance in a very short time.

WAKE UP
The following "wake up" procedure should be inserted at the end of your recording after you have finished giving suggestions.

Every time you enter hypnosis, you will be able to go under deeper better and faster as you learn to control your subconscious.

In a moment I will begin counting form one to five, and when I reach five you will open your eyes feeling wonderful and completely alert.

ONE - All faculties returning
.

TWO - Feeling refreshed and relaxed as everything returns to normal.

THREE - Returning to normal consciousness now.

FOUR - Beginning to move around some and stretching your body just a bit.

Now is the time for you to awaken. You will feel refreshed and relaxed and full of energy.

FIVE - Eyes open and wide awake. Take a deep breath now and stretch.

EFFECTIVE STRATEGIES

By its very nature, the subconscious mind must obey suggestions. During hypnosis, while the conscious mind is largely inhibited, it is possible to reach the subconscious with suggestions without influence by conscious interpretations of related memories and fixed ideas.

When you approach the subconscious without the interference of your conscious reasoning, you must follow certain rules in the wording of your suggestions. By structuring suggestions properly, you can put a great source of energy to work for you, carrying out your orders without the use of willpower or conscious effort of any sort.

Your subconscious is better at regulating your behavior than your conscious mind, because nature intended that as its function.

Most behavior is regulated on a subconscious level and any interference by your conscious mind is usually rather frustrating. The harder you try consciously to do something that your subconscious is supposed to do, the less chance you have to succeed. The insomniac can sleep only when he stops trying.

So, use the following principles in structuring your suggestions, relax, and let your subconscious do its job. It will never disappoint you.

1) The motivating desire must be strong.

Think of a reason - or a number of reasons - why you want your suggestion to be carried out. Start your suggestion with that motivating desire: "Because I choose to be attractive and slim, and enjoy better health," etc.

2) Be positive.

Never mention the negative ideas you intend to eliminate; repeat and emphasize the positive ideas you are replacing it with.

If you say, "My headache will be gone," you are suggesting a headache. You are claiming it as "Your Headache." This single mistake has caused many people to give up the use of hypnosis for self-improvement. Many times I have heard,

"Hypnosis won't work for me. I tried to use hypnosis to tell myself that I would not be fat, and I gained weight!" Well, the hypnosis did work. A badly worded suggestion instructed the subconscious to gain weight and be fat. Any suggestion - positive or negative - given under hypnosis, will work.

The trick is to word the suggestion so you get the desired result.

A proper wording of a weight suggestion would be, "I am a slim, trim, healthy and happy person, and I am always satisfied with a small meal."

A proper suggestion for the headache is, "My head is clear and relaxed and feels good."

Never mention or think about any idea that you are getting rid of. Self-hypnosis is positive thinking in its most practical form.

3) Always use the present tense.

As stated, the subconscious will always deliver what is asked of it. If you suggest, "Tomorrow I will begin to lose weight," the subconscious will wait for tomorrow to arrive before it begins to carry out the suggestion.

The problem is: tomorrow never arrives. It will wait and wait and wait. Our conscious reasoning mind has learned to speak of the future in the future tense. Since our subconscious is an emotional, feeling mind, it responds to the present only.

The proper wording is, "Every day I continue to lose pounds and inches as I progress toward my goal."

4) Visualize your suggestions.

As you give yourself suggestions, do not just say the words, think them, imagine them, and see yourself acting out the suggestion.

If your goal is to eliminate stage fright, feel and see yourself standing before a large crowd, speaking with poise and confidence. When you use your imagination, you are in direct contact with your subconscious. You must see yourself as you want to be or visualize your goal as already accomplished.

5) Suggest action, not ability to act.

Do not say, "I have the ability to dance well." Say, "I dance well, with ease and grace."

6) Exaggerate and emotionalize.

Your subconscious is the seat of your emotions. Exciting, powerful words and images will influence it. Use descriptive words such as wonderful, beautiful, thrilling, magnificent and tremendous! Say or think these words with feeling.

7) Use repetition.

When writing or formulating your suggestions, repeat it, enlarge upon it, and repeat it again in different words. The more exposure you have to an idea, the more it influences you.

EXAMPLE OF A
FINISHED SUGGESTION

First, you must select a goal. In this case, we will assume you want to lose weight. Now observe how this example follows the principle rules of suggestion.

DESIRE –
Because I have chosen to look and feel attractive and healthy, I eat only at mealtime and am satisfied completely with small meals.
POSITIVE –
I eat and enjoy only healthy foods. I eat slowly. Every day. I really do...
PRESENT TENSE –
...Look and feel better than the day before. Every day becoming a slimmer and healthier person.
REPETITION –
The pounds and inches just melt away.
ACTION –
I eat only at mealtime. I look and feel wonderful. I am attractive and ....
EMOTIONAL –
... It is thrilling to be noticed and to feel so beautiful (handsome).

HYPNOTHERAPY

There are times when a symptom or habit you consciously wish to eliminate plays a vital purpose in your life. Without realizing it, you may be dependent upon the symptom or habit for a defense against some traumatic situation you have chosen to forget.
In such cases, your subconscious may have difficulty accepting the desired suggestion. If the habit or symptom is causing enough discomfort or unhappiness to justify its removal, you might consider seeing a hypnotherapist who will take you
back to the time of the original trauma and uncover the event
you fear to face.

CHAPTER THREE

HYPNOSIS HELPS HEAL

Fear of hypnotism is gradually giving way to acceptance by a more enlightened society. In 1958, the AMA officially acknowledged the use of hypnosis by stating, "Hypnosis is a valuable and valid therapeutic tool." Psychiatrists are supplementing psychotherapy with hypnotherapy, often reducing the therapeutic process to less than one-eighth of the time formerly needed for a similar result.

Hypnosis, in and of itself, is not a cure for anything. It is, however, a valuable tool for helping the body heal itself. Under different names, hypnotic techniques are used for such things as controlling pain, stress management, and lowering blood pressure.

Our medical experts tell us that we often think ourselves sick, so it follows that by controlling and understanding the relationship between our thoughts and health, we might be able to think ourselves well.

Hypnosis is gaining acceptance in the area of law enforcement as indicated by the Florida decision allowing the use of hypnotically recalled testimony in court.

Hypnosis is valuable in all areas of behavior modification, such as weight control and stopping smoking. It has been used successfully to modify such habits as bed-wetting and nail biting, as well as phobia therapy. 46

STRESS MANAGEMENT

After the induction, insert the following script:

…And now as you continue to relax deeper into hypnosis you are going to eliminate stress from your life.

You always get enough sleep and rest.

You take a daily nap.

You set up a ritual that gives you regular hours of bedtime and avoid sleeping pills.

You get regular exercise.

Relaxed muscles mean relaxed nerves.

(Chose whatever exercise is realistic for your age and living condition: hiking, biking, golf, tennis, or home calisthenics)

You exercise on a daily basis.

You always avoid hurry and worry.

These are learned habits and can be unlearned.

You listen to your body.

You are learning to observe the warning signals such as tense neck muscles or gnawing in the stomach.

When your body gives these signals, back off and ease up.

You are not afraid to compromise.

In a stressful situation, you can either, fight, back off or compromise.

Seldom is the ideal situation available.

You do not use coping solutions that involve alcohol.

A little relaxation is fine, but drinking each time you are faced with a problem soon leads to alcoholism.

You always identify your fears, even list them.

Try to think of ways to cope with them.
Seek information about the things you fear.
Knowledge can bring runaway fears down to earth.
Once out in the open, the things we fear are seldom as terrible as we imagined.
You make decisions, right or wrong, and then act on them.
Anxiety results when you sit in the middle and your fears tug on you from opposite directions.
You laugh more.
Laughter is a good tension breaker.
Laugh at yourself so that you don't take yourself too seriously.
You avoid self-pity.
Self-pity is an immature and selfish response to situations and is always a waste of time and energy.
Now visualize a switch in your mind.
This is your stress switch.
Now see yourself reaching out and turning the switch to the off position.
As you turn the switch off, you feel all stress and anxiety leaving your body.
You feel calm and relaxed.
From now on, whenever you find yourself in a stressful situation, it is only necessary for you to turn off your stress switch.

CHILD BIRTH

These days, hypnosis is used more and more frequently for childbirth. My own daughter was delivered with hypnosis instead of chemical painkillers. With this method, my wife could be conscious and involved in the birthing process, and she managed labor in a more relaxed way.

When hypnosis is used to eliminate the discomfort of labor, the sensations and pleasant emotions of the experience are not impaired. Free of pain and anxiety, the mother is aware and can enjoy her baby's first cry. A qualified hypnotist should administer hypno-anesthesia. However, many women learn the art of self-hypnosis to manage their own pain, by managing labor in a more relaxed way. Self-hypnosis can be a tremendous help in preparing the mother for the big event by alleviating the fears and anxiety connected with childbirth, thereby making the delivery much easier. Most women have heard stories about how painful childbirth can be, and sometimes it seems as if friends and relatives make a special effort to tell you about the hardest part of their labors. Knowing the causes of pain in childbirth and understanding the purposes of the powerful sensations you feel make labor and birth easier and less frightening.

Using hypnosis to take the mother through a mental rehearsal for delivery also helps to eliminate fears. The mother feels like she has already gone through it and there is no need to worry; the less tension and fright, the easier the delivery.

This preparation brings a mother and baby together in a new way. The more joy there can be, the better for both. Here are suggestions for preparing an expectant mother for delivery:

As your breathing becomes more relaxed, let your thoughts drift inward, down, down, down to your uterus.
Picture your uterus… First from the outer layers…
It is a soft, smooth, deep pink group of muscles, snugly wrappings themselves around your baby.
Now look inside your uterus…
Picture your baby… Curled up… wet and warm…
Surrounded by the waters… floating… cradled by your pelvis…
Perfectly formed…
Look at the uterus from your baby's point of view…
The walls of the uterus lined with the silky soft membranes…
The placenta on the upper wall…
The umbilical cord leading to your baby…
Pulsating in rhythm with your body…
The air you breathe and the food you eat helping your baby to grow.
Now let yourself move forward in time… to the day your baby will be born.
You have felt your uterus contracting on and off all day long.
At first only mild contractions…
Now becoming more powerful.
With each contraction you breathe slowly and comfortably… taking energy deep into your body.
And each time you breathe out… tension flows away from you… leaving you renewed… strong and able to give birth to your baby.
The contractions are stronger…

Nudging your baby down... down... down... down into the cervix.
And you see the baby pressing into the cervix as it opens... opens... opens around your baby's head, and you relax and let your cervix open.

And now the contractions have taken on a greater strength... they have come and gone and the cervix is pushing your baby down... down... down deep into your vagina.
And you see your baby... wet and warm... and your vagina moist, soft, warm and elastic... massaging your baby.
And you open and open and let your baby come.
And your baby has reached the vaginal opening...
You feel the skin tingling... burning stretching... and you give your body time to open...
So you let the air out...
Lightly blowing... blowing as you feel the tissues stretch around your baby's head...
And finally the head slips out and you feel such relief...
And such pride and you rest...
And your baby begins to take in the world.
And the uterus contracts again... and you feel your baby turning to the side and the shoulders move under your pubic bone...
As you breathe, and the shoulders come out, there is a great release of pressure. As your baby slides out... and is taken and lifted onto your belly... you feel warm and wet and wonderful.

Now slowly come back to the present time... and feel your baby filling your uterus... not yet ready to be born... but knowing... just as you know how the journey will go in the future.

RELIEF OF PAIN

Hypnosis is effective as a medical adjunct, both as an analgesic and an anesthetic.

Hypnotic suggestions can alter the way messages of pain are perceived, processed, transmitted, and interpreted by the brain and central nervous system. From the temporary, localized pain experienced at the dentist's office, to the chronic pain of cancer patients, hypnosis offers new hope in alleviating suffering. Headaches, backaches, arthritis, rheumatism, menstrual cramps, labor pains and accident injuries are but a few of the many ailments that respond to the methods described in this book.

For more and more people, hypnosis is proving helpful in raising the threshold of pain and lessening the need for drugs.

Scientists have long been aware that the brain is the center of pain perception, and they are learning more every day. Among the newest information is the knowledge that the brain gives forth a morphine-like chemical responsible for the lessening of pain.

Imagine an incredibly potent painkiller available to everyone, able to relieve the most excruciating pain, with no harmful side effects.

Best of all, there is no fear of addiction. Your brain's chemistry is with you at all times, and this substance is two hundred times as powerful as morphine. It is called dynorphin - one of the families of the exciting brain chemicals called endorphins.

Evidence suggests that hypnosis releases endorphins from the brain during the trance state. The discovery that the brain can manufacture its own narcotic raises the real hope that we can diminish the use of addictive painkillers that have entrapped so many people.

Hypnotherapists believe that with successful application of the principles of hypnosis, the brain can be trained to produce extra secretions of its painkiller.

Your tolerance for pain can be raised in direct proportion to the relaxation of the muscles. Since anxiety leads to tension, it intensifies pain. Therefore, the total relaxation of hypnosis automatically raises the pain threshold.

When structuring your suggestions for pain control, keep in mind that the subconscious believes everything it is told. It controls the mechanisms that carry pain signals to the brain, the production of white corpuscles, and their transportation to the affected area. It can, therefore not only alleviate pain, but also may eliminate the cause as well.

The following suggestions need to be elaborated upon and repeated, but they carry the substance of the affirmation necessary for the general relief of both symptom and disease.

ARTHRITIS

Deposits of calcium between the bones at the joints cause arthritis.

Right now, with each movement you make, a drop of lubricant is secreted.

This natural lubricant is covering the calcium and allowing your joints to move in comfort.

At the same time, the lubricant is dissolving the calcium, and your condition is improving daily.

Your joints move in comfort because they are being lubricated.

The calcium is dissolving and you are feeling better every day.

You are now beginning to feel healing warmth flowing through the tissues of your skin.

The healing processes of your body are working right now... and you are feeling more comfortable and more at ease.

All pain, all discomfort, all swelling is diminishing flowing out of your body as easily and naturally as if it were being drawn from your body with a magnet.

All swelling is going down and all your joints are becoming normal in size.

SEE this happening;

VISUALIZE it in your mind's eye.

Your muscles are becoming stronger, yet they are loose and flexible.

The processes of your body are functioning properly now and healing your body perfectly.

BACKACHE

You should be extremely cautious when eliminating back pain. Pain is your body's way of telling you that something is wrong. If you block your back pain and decide you feel so good that you might as well go bowling, you are quite likely going to do more damage. You should use hypnosis to eliminate back pain only after your doctor has told you that there is nothing he can do and you will simply have to learn to live with it. With just a few sessions of self-hypnosis using the following suggestions, you should be able to live with it very well.

As you continue to relax, focus all of your attention on that part of your back that is giving you trouble. Concentrate on that area.

Now, imagine a brilliant beam of blinding white light striking that area of your back. You feel warmth spreading throughout the entire area.

The warmth intensifying… and now as the warmth begins to fade, you notice that the pain also fades.

Your back is feeling strong and comfortable.

Visualize yourself moving about, totally free of any pain or discomfort.

Your back is very strong and healthy.

You are now going to experience some very pleasant changes that will get rid of all the aches and pains in your back.

You are dissatisfied with the feeling of discomfort you have been experiencing and you want to get rid of those aches and pains now and forever.

It is natural for your body to be healthy. It is natural for all the bones in your back to be in perfect alignment. 55

It is natural for all the muscles in your back to be healthy and strong.

And is it natural for your subconscious mind to cause all of the activities of your body to function well and properly.
At this moment, your system is making comfortable adjustments.
it is pleasing to you to know your mind is causing your body to repair itself.
These repairs will continue to take place every day and night.
Every day you feel improvement as your mind causes your body to heal itself.
Feel the wonderful warmth of healing spreading throughout your back.

QUICK RECOVERY FROM DISEASE

When used with conventional medical care, self-hypnosis can speed recovery from any illness. Even terminal cancer patients surprise doctors by leading normal, pain-free lives for years by this method.
By following the guidelines in this chapter, you can structure your own suggestions to suit your individual needs.
The following is an example of the substance of the necessary suggestions:
Your body manufactures healthy cells that fight and kill harmful germs and bacterial.
Your body is manufacturing great quantities of these disease-fighting cells, and your arteries are transporting them to the areas where they are needed.
These healthy cells are killing the invaders and you are getting better every hour. Feeling better every hour.

This is just the skeleton of the suggestion. It must be repeated and enlarged upon. If, for instance, you have an infection, think of the infected area. Think of how it looks, and then visualize the antibodies doing battle, destroying the germs and replacing the diseased area with healthy flesh.

This affirmation and visualization, used properly with self hypnosis twice daily, will bring about dramatic results.

ENURESIS (BED-WETTING)

An enuresis problem may be caused by a physical condition, and if it is, no amount of hypnosis will solve the problem. However, if the original cause for the condition has been reinforced or replaced by a mental condition (fear/worry), then hypnosis can help.

The many worthwhile drugs used in the treatment of enuresis may fail if the physician does not include, along with his drugs, some needed reassurance and affirmations. If the hypnotist and the physician will work together, chances for overcoming the condition will be assured.

If you are making a tape or CD for a child, insert the following suggestions:

As you drift deeper into hypnosis, you can feel yourself growing.

You will soon be a grownup person.

You do want to grow up, don't you?

I know you want to grow up.

That is one of the reasons you want to stop wetting the bed.

You want to grow up and do things the way grownups do.

You want to graduate from school.

You want to drive a car.

And some day, you want to have your own home, and you sure want to stop wetting the bed.

Since you want to quit wetting the bed, I am going to tell you something that will keep you from ever wetting the bed again.

From now on, you will be able to sleep all night in a nice dry bed.

You are grown up enough now to always want to sleep in a nice dry bed just like grownups do.

You are old enough and smart enough that from now on, if you ever need to use the toilet during the night, you will wake up.

You will wake up and you will get out of your bed, and you will go to the toilet.

After you use the toilet, you will go back to bed and go back to sleep and sleep in a nice dry bed for the rest of the night.

Just before you go to bed each night, you will use the toilet and that will make it easier for you to go all night in a nice dry bed.

You will go to sleep in a dry bed and you will wake up in a dry bed.

You know that your bladder is made like a balloon so that it keeps stretching to hold the fluid all night long.

That lets you sleep comfortably all night long in a nice dry bed.

You are very happy and proud of yourself because you realize you are growing up.

You will be happier with your friends, and will be able to have your friends stay all night with you because you know that your bed will always be nice and dry.

If you ever need to use the toilet during the night, you will always wake up and go to the toilet.

And that way you will always sleep in a nice dry bed that you will be proud of.

Now that you don't wet the bed, you are more relaxed in school.

Your school grades improve more and more.

You are really proud of yourself.

CHAPTER FOUR

HYPNOSIS AND WEIGHT CONTROL

For most people, dieting is like sweeping back the ocean waves. As soon as the diet is over, the weight comes back.

A weight problem is the result of poor lifelong eating habits, and unless these habits are changed, any attempt at permanent weight control is futile.

People develop a weight problem as the result of a way of thinking, feeling and acting. Every person is the product of programming that has occurred throughout his or her entire life.

YOU ABSOLUTELY HAVE THE ABILITY TO CHANGE.

First, let us talk about some of the wrong programming. As children, we are given ideas and thoughts that we have no choice about at all. We accept them as valid at the time, though the ideas create problems for us later. Think about the following series of events that set our attitudes about food. Keep in mind that as children we have no choice but to accept these ideas and attitudes, but as adults we have an obligation to reject the old ideas that do not work.

What do you do when a baby cries? If it is not wet, you feed it. To the baby, something went into its mouth and it felt better. That sticks.

Later on, when a child falls down and skins a knee, they go running into the house with big tears streaming down their cheeks. If the magic kiss does not work, mom is stuck with a screaming kid. So, what does she do? She says, "Let's have some milk and cookies. That will make you feel better!"

What mom just did is known as "waking hypnosis." While in a highly emotional state, the child is told by mom - who is always right - that the milk and cookies will make them feel better.

A rule of mind is employed here: a person cannot focus on more than one thing at a time. With the child's mind now focused on the cookie, the pain goes away. Once again, mom was right. After this happens several more times, a habit pattern begins to form and before long, the child gets the idea: Milk and cookies make you feel good. 62

Later on, we learn that if we are really good we can have candy or ice cream. Now food becomes a reward or bribe. It follows that the opposite is punishment - going to bed without supper. Eating is a reward; dieting or cutting down is punishment.

As we get older, our parents bring out the heavy guns – guilt and sin. When children go through the finicky state, what do they all hear? "Eat everything on your plate. Think of the starving people in China." Somehow, the rest of the world will starve if you do not clean your plate.

As adults, we know that what we do or do not eat has nothing to do with politics. Nevertheless, when we eat there is still that little voice in the back of our mind saying, "Eat everything on your plate."

These are just a few of the wrong ideas that have been programmed into our minds since birth. Our parents did this to us because their parents did it to them and their parents did it to them. We must stop perpetuating these ideas.

When you use hypnosis to modify poor eating habits, you do not just lose a few pounds, but you can gain new positive attitudes that stay with you for the rest of your life.

Too many people confuse hunger with appetite. Appetite is a habit; hunger is a real need. Appetite is provoked by suggestion. Hunger is the message we receive when we need nourishment.

Compulsive eaters will strain their willpower and bypass their mind power. In other words, they consciously try to deny their appetite, instead of correcting the mental programming that causes them to crave unnecessary calories.

The body only does what the mind tells it to do.

With hypnosis, you can attain a healthy, normal weight and maintain it permanently while eating as much as you want. However, you will not want any more than your body needs.

To lose and maintain in this manner, use the following procedure:

Choose the ideal weight that you believe is right for you. Begin to visualize yourself at this ideal weight when practicing your self-hypnosis.

It will take practice, but this image of you is important.

As the subconscious begins to accept this new image of you, it will work 24 hours a day to fulfill that image. Visualize yourself standing in front of a full-length mirror, watching the pounds and inches melt away.

The following positive and beneficial ideas, fed into your computer-like subconscious during self-hypnosis, will free you from destructive eating habits while allowing you to eat without conscious restrictions.

To make the following nine suggestions easier to process, you might want to create a hypnotic tape or CD. You will first want to record the introduction method from Chapter Two. Say it slowly, in a soft voice. Then read the following affirmations and suggestions into the recorder, emphasizing the words you think are necessary.

Remember to repeat each suggestion several times. End the recording with the awakening procedure from Chapter Two.

Suggestions for Controlling Your Weight:

1) You only eat when you are physically hungry.

2) You eat only while sitting down (at a table). (This discourages eating on the run)

3) You are enjoying a new tasting habit.

Because you think only of the bite in your mouth, you enjoy the taste of it much more.

Your taste buds become more sensitive, and you get greater satisfaction from each bite.

You eat more slowly.

You eat much less - but you enjoy it more.

4) You enjoy drinking water.

You find it cool and refreshing.

5) You always leave some portion of each food on your plate. 64

6) You always lay your eating utensil down and think only of the bite that is in your mouth.
7) You avoid those foods that you know are bad for you.
8) You exercise more.
9) You are looking better and feeling better about yourself.

HYPNOSIS TO STOP SMOKING

If you have a strong desire to quit smoking, you can do it by using self-hypnosis. If, however, you are merely wondering if hypnosis can magically "make you quit," forget it.

Hypnosis cannot make you quit; it can only help you quit.

If you have a serious desire to shake the habit and be free, here is how you can do it:

1) Set a date.

Make a commitment to yourself that you will never smoke another cigarette after that date. It is best to give yourself a few days to get used to the idea that you will never smoke again.

During this period, tell your friends and relatives that they will never see you smoking after that date.

This is not just a matter of burning your bridges. Every time you tell someone that you are going to quit, you reinforce the idea in your mind that you mean what you say, and you strengthen your resolution to quit.

2) Practice being free from tobacco enslavement for short periods.

As your "tobacco freedom date" approaches, gradually cut down on the number of cigarettes you smoke.

During this time drink lots of water, and take long, deep breaths at least once every five minutes.

Most smokers only take a deep breath when they inhale. When they do not smoke, they miss these long deep breaths without realizing what they are missing.

A deep breath of clean air with its badly needed oxygen will give you part of the satisfaction you thought you were getting from the cigarette.

3) Listen to your hypnotic tape.

First, read the introduction method from Chapter Two. Record it slowly, in a soft voice.

Then read the following affirmations and suggestions into the recorder, emphasizing the words you think are necessary.

Remember to repeat each suggestion several times.

End the recording with the awakening procedure from the same chapter.

Suggestions for Breaking the Smoking Habit

And now as you continue to relax, you recall that at one time you had a reason to smoke.

It might have been because all of your friends smoked, or because you thought smoking was mature and sophisticated.

Whatever the reason you had, it was valid at the time, but times have changed.

Smoking is no longer socially acceptable and whatever reason you had is now invalid.

You have chosen to be a permanent non-smoker.

You thoroughly enjoy the feeling of complete freedom you get from knowing that you are a nonsmoker.

You feel so proud of yourself.

You have chosen life over death.

Strength over weakness.

You have a great new respect for your body.

You know that your lungs and your heart are the primary parts of your body that sustain the health and the energy you require to thoroughly enjoy living.

You respect and care for your lungs and your heart.

You have chosen health over sickness.

You are now free and you have broken the chains that bound you.

You are strong and intelligent enough to be a nonsmoker.

You have made a decision and you are now and forever a non-smoker.

You feel good about yourself, better than you have ever felt before.

You thoroughly enjoy breathing fresh, clean air.

The change your lungs have been gasping for.

That your body has been crying out for, has been made.

Long deep breaths make you feel good.

Take a deep breath now…

And as you exhale, relax and think the words "relaxed and free."

This is a wonderful feeling and with each breath you feel good all over.
Now, visualize yourself... Feel yourself as a healthy, happy non-smoker.
You are now free.
You feel better than you have felt for years, proud of your ability to conquer any habit.
Now go deeper. Let go even more.
And enjoy this pleasant relaxed feeling.
Imagine you are walking past a group of miserable people who are still sucking on their poison pacifiers.
Breathing in that body-poisoning smoke and blowing it out for others to breathe.
You don't hate them.
You don't even dislike them.

You understand them.
You understand their crippling weakness, so you tolerate them - poor things.
They can't help it. They are just stuck.
You sympathize with them.
But you are superior to these people.
You have a profound respect for your body.
You are now and forever a confirmed non-smoker.
Your final decision is made and agreed to, and every day that passes reinforces it.
Picture in your mind someone offering you a cigarette.
You always answer, "No, I have kicked the habit."
You might add, "I don't mind if you have one."
But you always say that you have kicked the habit.

Every time you refuse a cigarette, you feel a sense of power and pride.

You are proud of the fact that you have what it takes: guts, intelligence, self-respect and common sense.

You know that the longer you remain free of this repulsive habit, the easier it is to remain free, because you feel better with every day that it passes.

Better in body, mind and spirit.

You feel good all over.

You and you alone are in charge of your body.

You enjoy using this tape (or CD) and always feel invigorated and rejuvenated.

Just relax now and enjoy a moment of silence.

In a moment you will awaken....

Now insert the "wake-up" procedure here and you will come back to full awareness, feeling completely refreshed and proud of your ability to control your own behavior.

CHAPTER FIVE

SUCCESS

Success is the progressive realization of a worthwhile purpose or goal. What purpose or goal could be more worthwhile than a healthy and happy life?

You can use your mind to get rid of troubles, rather than attract them, and to achieve your every desire.

HOW SELF-DOUBT DEVELOPS

A complex is a deep-seated subconscious feeling, usually caused by a succession of disagreeable or misunderstood experiences.

These experiences have been pushed down into the subconscious mind and buried there. We say, "I have forgotten the experience and will have nothing more to do with it," yet the resulting feelings rise to the surface of conscious mind long after the original experience that caused them is forgotten.

As an illustration, let us say you make a mistake. You wish to be rid of the memory and, not understanding the way the mind works, you say, "That's over. I can't do anything about it. I'll put it out of my mind and never think of it again." You tell yourself
that you have forgotten it, but you have only dropped it into the subconscious.

Later, you make another mistake, and you drop it into your subconscious where it joins with the one already there --which you have not really forgotten. Other mistakes follow. All of these memories join together and form a guilt complex.

You may have had an experience of deep hurt. Perhaps you lost a member of your family upon whom you depended, or maybe you lost a fortune or a much-loved friend, and you feel rejected. You do not understand it. You feel wounded and you do not get over it. You drop the memory down into the subconscious.

Later, you have another hurtful experience and you drop that memory down into your subconscious where it attaches itself to the previous hurt. One hurt after another follows, until all those unhappy memories join to form a complex of rejection.

You think of life as unkind and everyone is against you.

These memories, repressed in the subconscious, are not forgotten; they continue to be active.

You may seem to be unable to meet life effectively and confidently, so you conclude that you are weak. You drop the memories of several unsuccessful experiences into the subconscious and you have an inferiority complex. These unresolved complexes block your successes in life – your happiness -- your faith in yourself.

Harmful complexes can be brought to the surface of conscious mind through psychological analysis. This is a good way of doing it, if the analyst is a good fisherman.

Another way is to pour love, good will, faith and happiness continuously into the subconscious. This will eliminate all harmful complexes.

To illustrate: Suppose you have a bottle of muddy water. There are two ways of replacing the muddy water with clear water. One, you can empty out all the muddy water and pour in clear water, or two, you can pour clear water on top continuously until all the water becomes perfectly clear.

DESTRUCTIVE EMOTIONS

Thinking with our emotions instead of our conscious or reasoning mind may be more comfortable, but we usually pay a heavy price for such comfort. The subconscious mind is supposed to be the servant that the conscious mind controls. An emotionally mature person learns to reject the emotions that are harmful to his well-being.

Such negative emotions include: anger, hostility, hatred, jealousy, anxiety and resentment. Positive emotions include love, friendship, kindness, forgiveness, generosity, sympathy, tolerance and charity.

The negative emotions make us unhappy and sick. The positive emotions keep up happy and well. It is as simple as that.

ANGER

Anger is the most destructive of all emotions because it lies hidden, unrecognized, inside many other symptoms. In guilt, we are angry with ourselves. In hatred, we are angry at the object of our hate. In self-pity, we are angry at the situations or people who frustrate us.

Expressed or suppressed, anger accounts for much of our misery. Few of us can become so emotionally mature that we completely free ourselves of anger. By

minimizing it, however, we can lead much happier lives. When we succeed in shaking
off the fetters of hostility, we replace anger with pity, and possibly even amusement.
We are exposed from the time of birth to anger-provoking situations. From the comfort of the womb, we are forced out into changing temperatures and hostile sounds. We are slapped on the bottom and wrapped in a dry cloth instead of the moist membranes to which we were accustomed. As we grow older, we are forced to drink from a cold, hard glass. Our anger mounts as we are required to delay natural functions until placed on a toilet seat. As more and more restrictions are heaped upon us, our frustration and anger increases.

Accepting these challenges and adjusting to them creates a person better conditioned to accept the responsibilities of adult life. Those who continue to rebel against the inevitable forces of nature and the necessary restrictions of group living become increasingly hostile towards others and towards themselves as well.
Expressing anger in relationships usually generates more anger and escalates hostility. Soon a vicious cycle is established and logical argument is replaced by foolish exaggerations and name-calling. Because of this, most people learn to suppress anger and thus it festers like an infected sore.
Those who repress or conceal their anger are in worse trouble than those who are emotionally immature. Since anger uses energy that must be released, this energy

surfaces in unpredictable ways. A man who will not talk back to his boss often finds an excuse to become angry with his wife. A woman may feel angry because of her seemingly thankless job of keeping house and raising children, and rather than accept the thought of anger, she suffers headaches or ulcers.

In these cases, the anger must be recognized and dealt with there is a great deal of good in life to counterbalance the bad. Although we must accept some of each, we can enjoy a minimum of the bad through improved thought patterns. We can change the inner-environment even if we cannot change the outer.

Suggestions for Controlling Anger

Because you want to live happily with others and enjoy both physical and emotional health, you have a feeling of peace and tolerance towards everyone.

You like people and people like you.

You realize each personality is the product of heredity and experience.

You know that if you had been born as someone else and had lived through their experiences you would act exactly as they do.

Therefore, you accept others as they are, and when they do things that you disapprove of, the only emotions you feel are sympathy and understanding.

You are in complete control of your emotions at all times. This gives you a feeling of great satisfaction.

You feel and express only the good, healthy emotions of love, kindness, sympathy and tolerance of others.

You love other people for their good qualities, and you forgive them for the acts you disapprove of, because you know that they are doing what you would do with their same body, experience, and level of awareness. You are a friendly and loving person, and you have a kind word and loving smile for everyone.

For this reason, you are well liked. Others like and admire you for your under-standing and forgiving nature.

Your subconscious mind is where the emotions reside, and it guides you in selecting good, healthy responses. You love others as they are.

You are in complete control of your emotions.

You radiate the good, healthy emotions and reject all others.

SELF-PITY

Acceptance is one of the keys to happy living. Positive action is the other. Change what you can, and then accept what you cannot.

The victim becomes stalled emotionally. He regards his own troubles as unique and believes he is getting more than his fair share of life's hardships. His troubles seem reason enough for his unhappiness.

Problems, hardships and disappointments are inevitable, but those who dwell on them invite more of the same.

We cannot deny the negative side of life, but we can learn to accept it as just one side of the coin.

The other side is the happiness we get if we reach out for it. The victim is self-centered. He must learn that he and his desires are not the center of the universe; he has his troubles and others have theirs.

Wanting things to be different is natural; to be unhappy if they are not different is self-destructive.

The victim uses suffering as a defense. They believe that if they evoke pity, they will be better liked.

Suggestions for Self-Pity

Because you want to live a happy and healthy life, and because you want other people to like you and enjoy your company, you accept life as it is and you accept people as they are.

You enjoy living more each day. You like people and you forgive them for not living up to your expectations.

You realize that there is a great deal of good in most people. You love people for their good qualities and forgive them for their mistakes.

You know the world has a lot of good to offer, and you concentrate on all the good things.

Therefore, you get the good things.

You reach out for happiness.

You find happiness because you anticipate it.

You look happy because you feel happy.

You smile when you greet your friends.

You have an enjoyable personality.

Being happy and contented with life brings you better health.

As you relax and accept life, your health improves daily and you feel wonderful.

GUILT

Guilt is a form of self-abuse. We punish ourselves by disrupting the vital functions of our body, inviting illness and depression.

The conscience is governed by the strength of the desire to conform to group customs.

A tribe in another country refuses to recognize a young warrior's manhood until he has killed a member of a neighboring tribe, so the young man's conscience is not at ease until he has committed what we consider cold-blooded murder. If we had been born in his environment, we would feel happy and proud after our first killing, so guilt is a relative matter.

How can you logically feel guilty about what your cultural experiences have made you? If you feel guilt, the act you feel guilty about is now a past experience. Feel sorry about what you have done, but not guilty, because like all other experiences, it caused a slight change in your total personality.

You are not the same person you were ten years ago. The minute you recognize a mistake and resolve not to repeat it, you have advanced your education and improved your character.

Consider your mistakes and experiences that served to enhance your future behavior. Do not feel guilty about something you would not repeat. If you feel regret, you have become a slightly better person as a result of your act.

You are forgiven automatically because you are not the same person who committed it. If you have to hate, hate the act that made you feel guilty, and do not repeat it.

A good rule of thumb is: If you would not do it again, you are forgiven.

To burden yourself with guilt is to misuse your brain by punishing those billions of hard-working cells that make up your body. You do not gain forgiveness by ruining the body entrusted to you.

Harboring guilt serves no purpose. It does not right wrongs and it does not help anyone or anything.

If you are using guilt as a form of self-punishment, you are breaking the laws of nature.

Everyone makes mistakes and you have the right to be wrong. You do not have the right to punish a healthy body and make it sick.

Suggestions for Feelings of Guilt

Because you want to have a healthy mind and a healthy body, you now forgive yourself for all things you have done in the past.

You remove a heavy burden from your shoulders as you forgive yourself and everyone else.

You want the best for everyone as well as yourself.

You are a loving person, and you live a happy, contented life.

You feel a great feeling of peace and tranquility as you forgive yourself and start with a clean slate every day.

You like yourself and people sense yourself respect.

You forgive yourself because forgiveness is good and right.

You are at peace with yourself and the world.

CHAPTER SIX

QUESTIONS AND ANSWERS

Q: What is hypnosis?

A: A state of hypnosis exists wherever we suspend the analytical thought process.

Q: Who can be hypnotized?

A: Every normal person experiences at least a light level of hypnosis every day of his or her life without realizing it. Even to enjoy a television show, radio program or a book, we must suspend critical thought. It is this capability of mind that allows us to identify with characters in stories and feel the emotions the actors are portraying. This is hypnosis in its most natural form. 100% of all normal people can and do experience hypnosis.

Q: What is meant by the conscious and subconscious mind?

A: Think of the mind as being divided into two parts, and although these two parts of mind work together, they have separate and distinct functions. The part of mind we are most aware of is the conscious mind. Scientists refer to this part of mind as beta level of thought. The conscious mind analyzes and labels all information we receive and then passes the labeled information along to the subconscious where it is stored.

The subconscious is by far the more powerful of the two levels of mind, although we are usually unaware of its operation. We call the subconscious the alpha level of thought. The subconscious is the source of our energy and motivation. No amount of willpower exerted by the conscious mind can override the subconscious.

Q: What are the functions of the conscious mind?

A: The conscious mind has a single function: to make critical judgments and decisions. It analyzes all information, and then passes that information along to the subconscious where it is filed in our mental computer. Although the conscious mind has the ability to reason and decide on a course of action, it cannot put a decision into action without the cooperation of the subconscious.

Q: What are the functions of the subconscious mind?

A: The subconscious mind has at least six basic functions:

(1) It permanently stores all memory -- everything we have ever heard, seen and tasted, smelled or felt.

(2) It controls all involuntary bodily functions, such as digestion and the immune system.

(3) It is the seat of our emotions.

(4) It is the home of our imagination.

(5) It controls all habitual conduct.

(6) It directs our energy.

Q: What is accidental hypnosis?

A: Accidental hypnosis is the automatic suspension of analytical thought, allowing random suggestions to be accepted and acted upon. Daydreaming is a good example of accidental hypnosis. This is the kind of hypnosis that renders us open to television programming.

Q: What is controlled hypnosis?
A: Controlled hypnosis involves the intentional suspension of the critical, analytical thinking process so that suggestions might be accepted for a specific purpose. Controlled hypnosis is done by either an operator / hypnotist or self-hypnosis.

Q: How does it feel to be hypnotized?
A: Most people remember everything that transpires while under hypnosis. A hypnotized person is not asleep. In most cases, the subject feels very relaxed and might experience a slight tingling sensation in either the hands or feet. There is no absolute feeling a person experiences. Many people report a very heavy feeling, while others report a light, floating sensation. Most people only become convinced they have been hypnotized after they begin to see the results of hypnotic programming.

Q: Is intelligence a factor in hypnosis?
A: Yes. The higher the intelligence, the better the subject. The better the mind, the better the individual's ability to take control of their analytical thinking process. The sharper the mind, the better the ability to concentrate, visualize and imagine. Therefore, intelligence is a factor, but not in the way most people suspect.

Q: Can people be hypnotized against their will?

A: Because all hypnosis is self-hypnosis, a person cannot be forced into a state of hypnosis. They can, however, become hypnotized without being aware it is happening. For example, we enter into a light state of hypnosis when we watch television, because we suspend analytical thought. When this happens, we are not aware of being hypnotized, but we are not being forced against our will either.

Q: Can people be made to do things they would not normally do?

A: Yes and no. A hypnotized person may do some things they would not normally do, but they cannot be made to do things they find morally objectionable. There are many things we would not consciously do because our inhibitions prohibit such actions. However, inhibitions are the result of critical thought, and when critical thought is suspended, so are our inhibitions. Morals, on the other hand, are more deeply imbedded into the personality and cannot be easily eliminated.

Q: Can a hypnotized person lose control?

A: Not only does the hypnotized person NOT lose control, they actually gain a degree of control. A person under controlled hypnosis has actually succeeded in controlling a function of mind -- critical thought – of which they generally have no control. Being able to turn off pain and change lifelong habit patterns is certainly evidence of gained control.

Q: Is hypnosis dangerous?

A: Absolutely not. Every person enters into a light level of hypnosis every day of his or her life. It is a natural state of mind. Furthermore, experiencing controlled hypnosis can be very healthy because many health problems are stress related. When analytical thought is suspended, stress is turned off.

Q: Why do some people fear hypnosis?

A: Fears are the result of faulty information. Understanding the true nature of hypnosis will eliminate such
fears.

Q: How do you know if you are hypnotized?

A: Usually, a person being hypnotized for the first time
will doubt they have been under at all. This is because
they did not feel they way they expected a hypnotized
person to feel. Most people only become convinced
after they begin to see the results from the hypnotic
programming, but an experienced hypnotist can tell if a
person is hypnotized simply by observing his subject.

Q: Is it possible not to come out of hypnosis?

A: No. By the very nature of hypnosis, it is impossible
for this to happen. In order to maintain itself, hypnosis is
dependent on outside stimuli. If a person is left in a
hypnotic state, he will eventually fall into a natural sleep
and awaken in a few minutes.

When you understand that a hypnotized person is not
truly asleep, you can understand that it is impossible for
him to "not awaken."

Q: Is it possible to be just a little hypnotized?

A: Yes. It is not necessary to be in a deep state to
receive the benefits of hypnosis. Many subjects do not
go deeper than a light to medium level, however, no
matter how deep a state, a person will respond to
suggestion.

Q: What can hypnosis cure?

A: Hypnosis, per se, will not cure anything. The medical
and psychological sciences are always on the watch for
new methods with which to alleviate discomfort and

promote the welfare of patients. It was in this spirit that the American Medical Association included hypnosis as a part of the progressive doctor's arsenal in 1958. Hypnosis is now accepted as a valuable therapeutic tool and is practiced by thousands of professionals worldwide.

Q: What do I have to do to be hypnotized?

A: First, you must put aside all preconceived ideas about hypnosis and keep an open mind. Also, you must be willing and have confidence in your hypnotist. Do not be analytical, simply relax and accept with confidence the suggestions given.

Q: Is there any objection to hypnosis on moral grounds?

A: It depends on the person's individual beliefs. Since one can never tell about the beliefs of others, we will tackle the question in general. Years ago, there was much discussion on the moral, ethical, and religious aspects of mesmerism (the forerunner of hypnosis). Some regarded the "trance" state as the healing gift of God, while others saw it as a threat. There are no longer any serious objections on such superstitious grounds. Greater knowledge has erased such criticism and science now knows there is no weakening of the will or domination of the subject from hypnosis. In fact, the first proclamation on this subject by the Roman Catholic Church came in 1847 and stated:

"Having removed all misconceptions, explicit or implicit invocation of the devil, the use of hypnosis is indeed merely an act of making use of physical media, and is not morally forbidden providing it does not tend toward an illicit end."

Q: What is self-hypnosis?
A: Self-hypnosis is simply the giving of suggestions to oneself, after having produced the receptive state of mind. Self hypnosis is an excellent method for positive, constructive and healthful conditioning. You can learn to tap abilities you do not even realize you possess.
Q: Will hypnosis tapes or CDs work as well as undergoing hypnosis with a hypnotist?
A: In most cases, yes. If you have specific goals you wish to accomplish with hypnosis, the results should be just as good with a recording as with a hypnotist -- and even better in some cases.

CLOSING COMMENTS

I hope you have found this overview of hypnosis to be both educational and enlightening. My goal with this brief text was to impart useful truths and dispel counter-productive myths about what hypnosis is and is not, and what it can and cannot do.
As I trust you have learned, hypnosis is quite a powerful tool that can help you to improve your quality of life in many, many ways. Yet, while the results may seem amazing, it is still a natural

phenomenon, not a mystical thing at all, and this fact may just be its greatest quality.

To learn more about practicing hypnosis and self-hypnosis for life improvement, Visit my Website : terrystokesshow.com

For Booking Information Contact:

Joy Turner
Entertainment Management Service
251-6261274

Mark Yuzuik is one of the most successful hypnotist I have ever trained. Mark took what I taught him and made it his own and in the process became one of my best friends.

I played The Calgary Stampede for 38 consecutive years. The crowds were always like this.

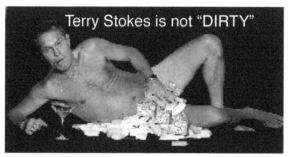

Terry Stokes is not "DIRTY"

When the Mandilay Bay in Las Vegas wanted to name my show "Dirty". I had this billboard made that proclaimed "Terry Stokes is not dirty". It actually only took one bar of soap to cover me...the others were just there for effect.

All in all, I would have to say....

IT HAS BEEN FUN!!!